WHITEWATER COOKS

at home

We wish to gratefully thank all the people who gave of their time and talents both in the kitchen and out:

Marianne Abraham, Petra, Chuck Corbin and Perri Bourree, Sue and Pat McLaughlin, Dale and Bob Boucher, Ali and Conner Adams, Olivia Ryan-Schmidt. Mia Fujibayashi, Yuki and Koko Conne, Nikko Fujibayashi-Lazier, Amelia Bressey Chapman. Emmy McKnight, Ellie McCallum, Anne Pigeon, Cottonwood Kitchens, Eryn Prospero Pottery, Heinz Laffin Pottery, Glory Vitug, Phil Schmidt, Christina Schnetzler, Geri Ryan, Gail Morrison, Linda Klein, Marie Weeks, Caroline Ryan, Caren McSherry, Karen Sowiak, Barb Gosney, Erin Bates, Nat Wansink, Gwen Cavanaugh, Marni Samychia, Sheri Weichel, Annie Bailey and Ryan Zsdany.

To all our recipe contributers we thank you and hope that you keep sharing.

Much thanks to our proofers: Marcia Hetherington, Caroline Ryan, Peter Lamb, Sabine Bos and Petra Bourree.

ISBN 978-0-9811424-0-1

All photographs except as noted copyright © 2009 David R. Gluns. All rights reserved. Email: david@gluns.ca

Photography: David R. Gluns
Food styling and recipe development/design: Shelley Adams and Joanne Ryan
Editing: Shelley Adams and Joanne Ryan
Back Cover Introduction: Sean McGinnis
Foreword: Mitchell Scott
Design and layout: Minn Benedict, Prefix Media - www.prefixmedia.com
Additional photographs: John Kernick and Bryan Ralph

Published by Shelley Adams, Nelson BC

Printed and bound in Canada by Friesens Book Division

Thanks to the owners of Whitewater Ski Resort: Dean Prodan, Mitch Putnam, Andrew Kyle.

To order a copy of this book, visit www.skiwhitewater.com
or www.whitewatercooks.com

WITH MUCH GRATITUDE, WE DEDICATE THIS BOOK

to the people of Nelson, who let Whitewater Cooks into their hearts and kitchens and made it a success.

Thanks to the local businesses who eagerly showcased Whitewater Cooks in their shops. And to our local grocery stores and markets for making even the most hard to find ingredients in our recipes readily available. You made it easy for people to explore new tastes at home.

Without all of your support this book would not have been possible.

CONTENTS

THERE IS A PLACE...

By Mitchell Scott

There is this place just up the road from town. Not too many people know about it, but at the same time, it is known. Its moniker travels widely, like the clouds do, through stories and rumours, legend and lore. Some think they know where it is, others have an idea, and then there are those who have given up careers, proximity to family and material wealth in order to live under its aura. It is small; a ski hill with only two, old, recycled, fixed gripped double chairlifts; at the base, a small, warm, utilitarian, half-buried lodge that tangs of ski boots, hot chocolate and yam fries. It is also big, this place. Mountains rise sharply and ridgelines spread into every corner of the distance.

Full of nooks and crannies, there seems to be a name for every tree and knoll, chute and bowl. The best run is right under the lift, the classic old school ripper, where locals holler for face shots and air. They call you by your name. They erupt when you rip and bellow when you lose control, pushing you through burning thighs and loss of breath.

Here, the snow falls deep and light and dry. Summer thinned stashes are hidden by walls of cedar boughs. Touring packs lie in heaps at the top of the lift. Telemarkers, snowboarders and skiers cruise about the lodge with toque-matt hair. When the sun shines, liftees cook sausages at the top lift shack and play electric guitar through beat-up amplifiers. Adorning all, transceivers hang from permanently scented Polypropylene chests. Red lights transceiving stoke...vibrancy...excitement...life.

One grooming machine tries to keep up with epic snowfall—anywhere between 30 to 50 feet a year. One grader for the six-mile access road. The machine shack is manned by one mechanic, a fellow whose beard is as long as the wrench he yields—the stories he tells. The head of lift operations takes rights to early morning powder runs instead of a raise. He also keeps a snorkel in the lift shack...just in case. He calls his dog Mogul and has a fence around his yard made of old skis. The director of snow safety used to be a star in ski magazines and films. He sends it bigger than anyone on the hill.

Trucks carry packs of riders back from backside stashes. Hour-long walks deliver huge, aggressive runs that spin back to the lodge. The lodge, where ski boot worn wood and picnic table décor play host to red-cheeked kids and their powder afflicted parents. Where hearty, wholesome, ridiculously delicious food fuels neverending adventure.

The road winds and twists through snow banks and ditched cars. If you're lucky, you make it up before the local school bus gets stuck, the sure fire recipe for low-density powder mornings. People rally through grill high two hours before the hill opens just to get first chair. Only one phone line makes it up to this place, reserved only for emergencies. Hidden at the end of a steep-walled valley where cell phones display "No Service," if you want to call your friends to tell how epic the day is, quite simply, quite romantically, you can't.

Cars get stuck in the parking lot at the end of the day because it has snowed so much. Skiers complain of having to suffer through sore ankles, knees, and backs because the snow just won't stop. They just can't stop. A place where ski patrollers rip underneath the chair, throwin' 360's and grabs and backscratchers. Where every couple of years or so the snow under the chairlift becomes so deep the mountain has to hire a full-time shovelling crew just to keep it running.

At this place, just up the road from town, there hides a gem, some days more than others. A place where smiles break through snow encrusted goggles. Where people shred away the burdens of the world. Friendship and family forged over powder and good times. There are no high-speed quads. There probably never will be. Things are good the way they are. No fancy hotels. No high priced real estate. Just skiing pure, distilled, for the community, for friends, for whoever finds it. For whoever is willing to bundle up and submit to it.

It's special because it is something, not trying to be something. It has found the balance that rules everything from galaxies to weather systems. A place where the more you experience it, the more it becomes you, the more you become it.

Symbiosis discovered by skiing. Fast but slow. Small but big. Deep but cheap.

STARTERS

PROSCIUTTO AND BASIL WRAPPED PRAWNS

These may seem tricky the first time you make them but you will be well rewarded for your effort. Don't even attempt with small prawns though, or you'll drive yourself crazy.

- MAKES ABOUT 20 -

INGREDIENTS

1 bag large raw prawns 16/20 count (454 g)

200 g thinly sliced prosciutto

1 bunch fresh basil

1 1/2 cups (375 ml) panko bread crumbs

1/4 cup (60 ml) parmesan cheese, grated

2 tbsp (30 ml) chopped parsley

1/2 tsp (2 ml) black pepper

1/2 cup (125 ml) olive oil

1/2 cup (125 ml) vegetable oil

1 lemon, quartered

METHOD

Thaw and peel prawns leaving the tail on.

Soak the prawns for about 20 minutes in some cold salted water, drain and pat dry.

Slice each piece of prosciutto into 2 or 3 (depending on the size) lengthwise slices. You want to keep the pieces long for wrapping.

Separate the basil leaves from the stems, keeping the largest, and reserving the smaller leaves for another use. If the leaves are really big cut them in half lengthwise.

Combine the panko crumbs, parmesan cheese, chopped parsley and pepper in a small bowl.

Pour the olive oil into a small bowl.

Dip your fingers a little into the olive oil and start to wrap the prawns, basil first then prosciutto. The oil should help things adhere and enable you to get a nice snug wrap.

Brush or rub a little more olive oil on the wrapped prawns and roll and press them into the crumb mixture.

Place all the prawns in a container, tightly packing them, sprinkle with any remaining crumbs.

Cover the container with plastic wrap and refrigerate for at least an hour and up to 24 hours.

Heat vegetable oil in a large frying pan to medium high heat.

Sauté the prawns, turning once (in batches if you have to) until golden brown on both sides. About 3 minutes on each side.

Serve right away with some lemon wedges

These are one of our most requested appetizers for both family events and catering jobs. We used to kind of dread making them for large parties until we realized that they could easily be prepared the day ahead (the crust even seems to adhere a little better when refrigerated overnight). So we still make them and often, because people love them and we love that.

CARAMELIZED ONION AND GORGONZOLA TARTS

This delectable appetizer comes from our friend Marianne who has years of cooking and catering under her apron strings...

- SERVES 6 (BASED ON 2 EACH) -

INGREDIENTS

4 medium white onions, thinly sliced
1/4 cup (60 ml) maple syrup
1/4 cup (60 ml) brown sugar
1/4 cup (60 ml) balsamic vinegar
1 tsp (5 ml) salt
2 tbsp (30 ml) olive oil
1 head garlic
1 (397 g) package puff pastry, defrosted
egg wash, 1 yolk beaten with 2 tbsp (30 ml) water
1 cup (250 ml) mozzarella, grated
1/2 cup (125 ml) asiago, grated
1 cup (250 ml) gorgonzola or blue cheese, crumbled

METHOD

Preheat oven to 325°F (160°C)
Combine onions, maple syrup, brown sugar, balsamic vinegar, salt and olive oil in a large bowl. Spread the onion mixture out onto a large shallow baking sheet. Cover with foil. Wrap up the head of garlic in a little piece of foil. Put the onion mixture and the garlic in the oven for two hours. Take the garlic out after one hour.
Remove the onions from oven, take off the foil and let cool completely. When the garlic can be handled, squeeze the soft flesh out of each clove into a small bowl and mash with a fork.
Roll out each block of pastry into a 12x7 inch (30x17 cm) rectangle.
Cut each piece into 8 squares and place on two parchment lined baking sheets. With your fingers, roll the corners and edges of each square and crimp with a fork. Brush the edges with the egg wash.
Spread each square of puff pastry with mashed garlic, staying within the crimped edges. Put about 2 heaping tbsp (30 ml) of caramelized onions on each piece, spread mozzarella and asiago on top of onions and then sprinkle with blue cheese. Put the pastries (on the sheet pan) in the freezer for at least 15 minutes or cover and freeze until you need them.
Bake in a 400°F (200°C) oven until puffed and golden brown (about 25 minutes).
Serve right away.

These tarts freeze beautifully. Leave them on the baking sheet without overlapping any pieces and put the sheet in the freezer. Once they are frozen, the tarts can be removed and stacked into containers or freezer bags. Think how smug you'd be if you could pull these beauties out of your freezer and present them to your guests in half an hour.

CAPRESE WITH FRESH SHRIMP

This is the classic combination of bocconcini and tomatoes with a west coast twist. Shelley's daughter Ali, came up with this version one day when she was craving something healthy, fresh and quick.

- SERVES 4 TO 6 -

INGREDIENTS

1 pint (475 ml) container cherry or grape tomatoes, cut in half
1 cup (250 ml) mini mozzarella balls (bocconcini) or large ones cut in equivalent size to the tomatoes
1 cup (250 ml) fresh shrimp, hand peeled if possible
1/4 cup (60 ml) fresh basil, julienned
2 tbsp (30 ml) fresh dill, chopped
1/4 cup (60 ml) extra virgin olive oil
1 tsp (5 ml) sea salt
1/2 tsp (2 ml) black pepper
juice of 1/2 lemon

METHOD

Mix together, tomatoes, bocconcini, shrimp, basil, dill, olive oil, sea salt, pepper and lemon juice and place in your prettiest bowl or platter.
Serve surrounded with Marie's Rosemary Nut Crackers or a sliced crusty baguette.

This is really good without the shrimp too, and perfect for bringing to a beach party.
Marie's Rosemary Nut Crackers can be found on Page 22.

BEEF TENDERLOIN AND CAMBOZOLA CONES

This is an elegant appetizer and a good way to share a beautiful cut of meat with your friends. The richness of the beef will sustain even the heartiest of appetites until dinner is served.

- SERVES ABOUT 8 -

INGREDIENTS

2 tbsp (30 ml) soy sauce

2 tbsp (30 ml) olive oil

1/4 cup (60 ml) white wine vinegar

1 lb (500 g) beef tenderloin fillet, trimmed

2 tbsp (30 ml) salt

8 oz (250 g) cambozola cheese, room temperature

2 tbsp (30 ml) butter, room temperature

1 tsp (5 ml) black pepper

30 arugula leaves, trimmed

1/4 cup (60 ml) horseradish

1/2 cup (125 ml) sour cream

METHOD

Whisk together the soy sauce, olive oil and white wine vinegar and pour over beef, cover and marinate in a non-reactive dish for at least an hour, or up to overnight.

Preheat your oven to 375°F (190°C).

Remove from marinade and salt generously.

Sauté in ovenproof pan on high heat searing all sides of beef until nicely browned (about 1 minute per side).

Put beef in oven and roast for about 20 minutes more. Remove from oven and let cool. If time permits, refrigerate beef thoroughly, as it is much easier to slice thinly when cold.

Mash and blend together the cambozola, butter and pepper.

Slice the beef as thinly as possible.

Place a spoonful of the cambozola and butter mixture at the edge of each slice of beef. Roll the beef around the cheese and into a cone shape. Just before you get to the end, insert an arugula leaf so that it sticks out the top of the cone.

Mix together the horseradish and sour cream in a small bowl.

Arrange the cones on a platter with the bowl of horseradish cream in the middle as a dip.

This dish along with a salad and a loaf of crusty bread from Au Soleil Levant Bakery would make a simple and decadent lunch.

AHI TUNA TARTARE WITH CRISPY WONTONS

The combination of the cool, fresh tuna and crispy wonton is out of this world. This is an extravagance, as ahi tuna is a pricey treat, but sometimes a little extravagance is what it's all about.

- SERVES 6 (BASED ON 2 EACH) -

INGREDIENTS

About 25 wonton wrappers (mandarin brand are best)
1 1/2 cups (375 ml) vegetable oil
3/4 lb (about 375 g) fresh ahi tuna, diced in small cubes
1/4 cup (60 ml) mayonnaise
1 tbsp (15 ml) sweet red chili sauce
2 tsp (10 ml) sesame oil
2 tbsp (30 ml) green onions, chopped
1 tbsp (15 ml) pickled sushi ginger, finely chopped
1/4 cup (60 ml) fresh cilantro, chopped
1 tsp (5 ml) wasabi powder
1 tbsp (15 ml) tamari or soy sauce
1/4 cup (60 ml) toasted sesame seeds
cilantro sprigs for garnish
2 tbsp (30 ml) pickled sushi ginger, chopped

METHOD

Heat oil in a heavy deep pan over medium high heat until hot but not smoking.
Drop one wonton wrapper in the oil. If it sizzles and turns golden brown in about a minute the oil is ready. Fry wontons a few at a time, flipping to lightly brown and crisp both sides. Drain on paper towel.
Combine mayonnaise, chili sauce, sesame oil, green onions, sushi ginger and cilantro in a medium sized bowl.
Whisk together wasabi powder and tamari. Add to mayonnaise mixture.
Add tuna and stir gently until just combined.
Cover and refrigerate until ready to use. To assemble, place a spoonful of tuna mixture on each wonton and garnish with toasted sesame seeds, cilantro sprigs and pickled sushi ginger. Or put the tartare in a pretty bowl surrounded by the crisps and let your guests help themselves.

These wonton crisps are a really fun and different way of serving any number of things. They can also be made ahead and stored in an air tight container for up to one week. We often serve them with our Shrimp and Mango Salad on Page 61.

GRILLED FRESH FIGS WRAPPED IN PROSCIUTTO

We can find fresh figs here locally in late august and through september. So if you come across them in your local farmer's market or anywhere, buy them right away and make this!

- SERVES 4 (BASED ON 3 PER PERSON) -

INGREDIENTS

6 fresh figs
100 g thinly sliced prosciutto or approximately 6 pieces
8 oz (250 g) cambozola cheese
1 cup (250 ml) balsamic vinegar
1/4 cup (60 ml) honey
1/4 cup (60 ml) port wine
6 cups (1.5 L) arugula or spicy greens

METHOD

Cut figs in half lengthwise. With a teaspoon, pull apart and make room for the cheese.
Place about a teaspoon of cheese in each half fig.
Slice each piece of prosciutto in half lengthwise.
Place fig at the bottom end of the strip and roll up snugly, covering all the cheese. Put a toothpick in each bundle to hold it together.
Combine balsamic vinegar, honey and port in a saucepot and simmer on medium heat until reduced in volume by 1/3. You should have roughly 3/4 cup (175 ml) of dressing. Let cool slightly.
Grill figs on medium barbeque until proscuitto is brown and crisp, about 5 minutes.
Serve figs on a bed of arugula or spicy greens and drizzle with the warm balsamic dressing.

You can also serve these beautiful figs simply stuffed with a little blob of cheese and drizzled with the dressing, especially if the crowd includes a few vegetarians. This appetizer is an amazing start to any summer or fall dinner.

CRUDITÉS WITH A NUTTY MISO DIPPING SAUCE

This is so easy to make and serve. Use whatever pretty clear glass containers that you like. Pour the sauce into the bottom then put the crudités in standing up. Cut your vegetables in suitable lengths to fit in to whatever glassware you choose for this unique presentation.

- SERVES 6 -

INGREDIENTS

1 1/2 lbs (750 g) vegetables such as asparagus, green beans, carrots, and cucumbers. Any kind of fresh seasonal vegetable.

1 garlic clove, minced
1 tsp (5 ml) fresh ginger, finely grated
1 tbsp (15 ml) miso paste
1 tbsp (15 ml) dijon mustard
2 tbsp (30 ml) soy sauce
2 tbsp (30 ml) rice wine vinegar
1 tbsp (15 ml) sesame oil
3/4 cup (175 ml) vegetable oil
1/2 cup (125 ml) toasted sesame seeds
1/2 cup (125 ml) almonds, toasted and roughly ground
2 tbsp (30 ml) toasted sesame seeds for garnish

METHOD

Snap the tough ends of the asparagus and peel the bottom 1 inch (2.5 cm) if desired.
Blanch asparagus for about 2 or 3 minutes.
Plunge into cold water to stop the cooking.
Wrap in tea towel and keep in the fridge until ready to serve. Use the same method for the green beans. Carrots and cucumbers should be julienned to fit the container you choose and can be served raw.
Make the dressing by mixing together the garlic, ginger, miso paste, dijon, soy sauce, vinegar and sesame oil.
Pour the vegetable oil in slowly, whisking until emulsified.
Whisk in toasted sesame seeds and ground toasted almonds.
Place some of the dressing into the bottom of the serving container and arrange the crudités standing up to fill the container. Sprinkle with sesame seeds.

They look beautiful all in a row on a summer table, or passed around with a cocktail...

CHICKEN SKEWERS WITH RUM AND PEPPER PAINT

Always a party favourite and for good reason. It's both easy on the cook and tasty. Marinate the chicken overnight and make the spicy pepper sauce the day before. All you need to do when your guests arrive is fire up the barbeque.

- SERVES 4 TO 6 -

INGREDIENTS

6-6 inch (15 cm) wooden skewers
1 lb (500 g) boneless, skinless chicken thighs
juice and zest of 1 lemon
2 cloves garlic, minced
1/2 medium onion, grated
1 small red chili, minced (reserve a little for garnish)
1 cup (250 ml) cilantro, chopped
1/2 tsp (2 ml) salt
1/3 cup (75 ml) olive oil

FOR RUM AND PEPPER PAINT

1 tbsp (15 ml) whole black peppercorns
4 whole cloves
1/4 cup (60 ml) sugar
1/2 cup (125 ml) soy sauce
1/2 cup (125 ml) light rum
2 tbsp (30 ml) lemon grass, chopped
juice and zest of 1 lemon

METHOD

Soak the skewers in water to prevent them from burning on the grill.

Trim the chicken of excess fat and cut into 1 inch (2.5 cm) pieces.

Whisk together the lemon juice and zest, garlic, onion, chili, cilantro, salt and olive oil. You could put everything in a food processor and give it a quick whir to combine it if you like.

Put the chicken in a sealable container and pour the marinade over, covering all the pieces of chicken. Cover and refrigerate for a couple of hours or overnight.

Make the Rum and Pepper Paint by toasting the peppercorns and cloves in a dry skillet for a minute. Grind them in a spice grinder or mortar and pestle until coarsely ground. Put all other ingredients and the spices into a small pot and bring to a simmer on medium high heat.

Simmer for about 20 minutes until it has reduced by about half. Strain through a fine sieve and set aside.

Thread the chicken pieces securely onto the skewers.

Heat the barbeque or a grill pan to medium high heat.

Sprinkle the chicken skewers with salt and pepper and grill for about 5 to 6 minutes on each side until fully cooked and golden brown.

Serve drizzled with the Rum and Pepper paint and put the remainder in a little dish for dipping.

Garnish with the reserved chopped red chili and some fresh cilantro.

This marinade is a good starting point. Add whatever fresh herbs you have on hand or growing in the garden. Mint and parsley are especially good.

PANKO CRUSTED OYSTERS WITH NEW WAVE TARTAR SAUCE

We can get beautiful B.C. oysters here in Nelson and there is almost nothing better than a plump crispy oyster with some zippy tartar sauce.

- SERVES 4 -

TARTAR SAUCE

1/3 cup (75 ml) mayonnaise

1/3 cup (75 ml) plain yogurt

1 tsp (5 ml) dijon mustard

2 tbsp (30 ml) fresh dill, finely chopped

1 tbsp (15 ml) capers, chopped

1/4 cup (60 ml) cucumber, finely diced

1 tbsp (15 ml) lemon juice

INGREDIENTS

one 8 oz (240 ml) container shucked oysters (about 8)

1/4 cup (60 ml) cornstarch

1/4 cup (60 ml) water

3/4 cup (175 ml) panko (japanese bread crumbs)*

1/4 cup (60 ml) parsley, finely chopped

1 tsp (5 ml) salt

1 tsp (5 ml) black pepper, freshly ground

1 tsp (5 ml) paprika

1/4 cup (60 ml) vegetable oil for frying

METHOD

Whisk together all ingredients for the tartar sauce and refrigerate until needed.

Drain the oysters in a colander.

Whisk together the cornstarch and water in a small bowl.

Combine the panko, parsley, salt, pepper and paprika in another bowl.

Dip the oysters in the cornstarch and water mixture and then roll them in the crumbs, pressing lightly to coat well.

Heat oil in a large frying pan to medium high heat.

Put the oysters carefully in the hot oil (they may spatter a bit).

Cook for about 3 to 5 minutes on each side (depending on their size) until golden brown.

Serve with a wedge of lemon and a dollop of tartar sauce.

These make a great appetizer or a quick lunch or brunch for two. Just toss a little salad and serve the oysters on top. A glass of beer perhaps and the Sunday paper…

*Panko are the Japanese version of "bread crumbs". They are lighter and flakier than regular bread crumbs, and are particularly good for coating seafood as food tends to stay crispier and absorbs less grease. Panko can be used just as you would regular bread crumbs in all your recipes. Tossed with a little seasoning, melted butter and cheese and you have the ultimate crispy topping for casseroles. Available locally at the Kootenay Co-Op.

POTATO AND FRESH ROSEMARY FOCACCIA

This is such a delicious version of foccacia. The mashed potatoes make it chewy, airy and flavourful. It's one of our all time favourites and it's sure to become one of yours.

- SERVES 12 -

INGREDIENTS

1 lb (500 g) potatoes, peeled and chopped
1 1/2 cups (375 ml) reserved potato water
1 tsp (5 ml) active dry yeast
1/2 tsp (2 ml) white sugar
4 to 4 1/2 cups (950 ml) all purpose unbleached flour
1 tsp (5 ml) salt
2 tbsp (30 ml) cornmeal
1 tbsp (15 ml) olive oil
1 tbsp (15 ml) fresh rosemary, chopped
2 tbsp (30 ml) coarse sea salt

This bread can be topped with so many different things before baking. Here are some of our favourites...

Crumbled feta or goat cheese
Any kind of olives (you need to press them into the dough)
Sun dried tomatoes
Fresh roma tomatoes and thyme
Prosciutto
Artichokes
Grapes and pine nuts

METHOD

Boil the potatoes until tender.
Drain taking care to reserve the potato water. You will need 1 1/2 cups (375 ml) of water.
Mash the potatoes and set aside. You will need about 2 cups (500 ml), mashed.
Pour the lukewarm potato water into a large bowl. If it becomes too cool, reheat it in the microwave until lukewarm again.
Whisk the sugar and yeast into the lukewarm water and let proof 8 to 10 minutes until foamy.
Mix potatoes into yeast mixture with a wooden spoon or whisk.
Mix in flour and salt until combined. Mixture will be quite sticky.
Pour out onto a floured surface and knead for 6 to 8 minutes until it becomes smooth and elastic. The dough will remain somewhat sticky.
Oil a large glass or ceramic bowl and place dough in the bowl and roll it around until it's coated.
Cover with plastic wrap and refrigerate overnight. You can also put it in a large, strong, oiled resealable plastic bag.
Remove the dough from the fridge the following day and place on a lightly floured surface and punch down.
Oil a 13x18 inch (33x45 cm) baking pan and sprinkle with cornmeal.
Roll out and place on the prepared pan. You'll have to pull the dough out and stretch it to completely cover the pan.
Cover with a tea towel and let proof in a warm place for 45-60 minutes.
Rub olive oil over the surface. Sprinkle with rosemary and sea salt.
Bake for 45 minutes at 350°F (180°C)
Cool on a rack before cutting.

RUSTIC TOMATO TARTS

These simple, delicious and versatile tarts are one of our summertime entertaining stand-bys. Make them in the cool of the morning and serve them at room temperature or warmed up a little on the barbeque at any time of day. We like them best on the dock in the late afternoon with a cold glass of sauvignon blanc... and one more swim before dinner.

- MAKES 2 TARTS. EACH TART SERVES ABOUT 4 AS AN APPETIZER -

CORNMEAL DOUGH

¼ cup (60 ml) sour cream
¼ cup (60 ml) ice water
1 cup (250 ml) flour
⅓ cup (75 ml) cornmeal
½ tsp (2 ml) salt
½ cup (125 ml) cold butter cut into cubes

TOPPING

6 medium tomatoes, thinly sliced
10 oz (300 g) soft goat cheese, crumbled
1 big bunch basil, roughly chopped
½ cup (125 ml) parmesan, grated
1 tsp (5 ml) pepper, freshly ground

We almost always double the dough part of this recipe and freeze or refrigerate the extra, then all you need is a few minutes effort to create any number of delicious, sweet and savoury tarts.

Some of our favourites are:
asparagus and fontina cheese
caramelized onion and gorgonzola
fig, prosciutto and cambozola
pear, almond, and chocolate

METHOD

Stir the sour cream and ice water together in a small bowl.
Put the flour, cornmeal and salt in a mixing bowl and stir with a whisk.
Add the cold butter and work it into the dry ingredients with a pastry blender or your fingers, till you have a nice crumbly mixture.
Add the sour cream mixture all at once to the dry ingredients, with a fork. Your dough will form a loose ball and will probably seem too moist, but just mix it together gently and separate it into two even disks. Use some flour on your fingers to keep it from sticking.
Wrap in plastic wrap and place in the fridge for at least two hours.

Put the sliced tomatoes on a couple of sheets of paper towel or a tea towel to drain a bit of the moisture out of them. This will prevent your tarts from becoming soggy.
Mix together the crumbled goat cheese and the basil in a small bowl.
Roll out each disk of dough on a well-floured board. Don't get too hung up about the shape of your dough, just roll it to about 11 inches (27.5 cm), more or less round.
Place each piece of dough onto a cornmeal sprinkled pan that has been lined with parchment paper.
Scatter the goat cheese and basil onto the rolled out dough leaving a 1 inch (2.5 cm.) border. Arrange the tomatoes on top of the cheese somewhat prettily.
Sprinkle with the parmesan and the pepper.
Fold the edges of the tarts up to form small folds along the edge of the dough. Gently press down with your fingers. Once again don't get too worked up about things, the look you're going for here is rustic.
Bake the tarts in a 375°F (190°C) oven for about 30 minutes until they are crisp and golden brown. You may have to rotate them in your oven for even baking.
Slide the tarts out onto a cooling rack and try to let them rest for at least 5 minutes before cutting into slices like a pizza.

MARIE'S ROSEMARY NUT CRACKERS

Our friend Marie Weeks came up with this delightful version of a popular cracker. Paired with your favourite cheese, these are scrumptious yet light and healthy. Makes a fairly big batch but freezes beautifully.

- MAKES 60 TO 75 CRACKERS -

INGREDIENTS

2 cups (500 ml) flour

2 tsp (10 ml) baking soda

1 tsp (5 ml) salt

2 cups (500 ml) buttermilk

1/4 cup (60 ml) brown sugar

1/4 cup (60 ml) honey

1 cup (250 ml) raisins

1/2 cup (125 ml) pecans, toasted and chopped

1/2 cup (125 ml) roasted pumpkin seeds

1/4 cup (60 ml) sesame seeds

1/4 cup (60 ml) flaxseed, ground

2 tbsp (30 ml) parmesan cheese, grated

2 tbsp (30 ml) fresh rosemary, finely chopped

METHOD

Preheat oven to 350°F (180°C).

Stir together the flour, baking soda and salt in a large bowl. Add the buttermilk, brown sugar and honey and stir until just combined.

Add the raisins, pecans, pumpkin seeds, sesame seeds, flaxseed, parmesan and rosemary and stir just until well blended. Pour the batter into two 8x4 inch (1.5 L) greased loaf pans.

Bake for about 35 minutes or until golden and springy to the touch.

Remove from the pans and let cool on a wire rack. The cooler the loaf the easier it is to slice really thin. You can leave it to cool in the fridge overnight if you like.

Slice the loaves as thin as you can and place the slices in a single layer on an ungreased cookie sheet.

Bake them in a 350°F (180°C) oven for 10 minutes, then flip them over and bake for another 10 minutes until crisp and deep golden in colour.

Remove from the pan and let cool completely on a wire rack.

Store in a cookie tin or freeze in sealed containers.

There are so many things to serve with these addictive crackers. Our Goat Cheese and Sun-Dried Tomato Terrine on Page 28 would be a fabulous pairing at your next dinner party.

CHICKEN QUESADILLAS WITH PUMPKIN MOLE SAUCE

We made these for a big backyard garden party a few years ago. It was a hot summer night, the mojitos were flowing and these quesadillas were devoured as quickly as they came off the grill.

- SERVES 8 TO 10 -

MOLE SAUCE

1/2 cup (125 ml) unsalted pumpkin seeds

1/2 cup (125 ml) unsalted peanuts

2 tbsp (30 ml) olive oil

1 medium onion, diced

2 cloves garlic, minced

one (127 ml) can green chilies, drained, and seeded**

1 tbsp (15 ml) canned chipotle in adobo sauce*

1 tsp (5 ml) cinnamon

2 tsp (10 ml) chili powder

2 tsp (10 ml) cumin

1/2 tsp (2 ml) salt

2 tbsp (30 ml) maple syrup or brown sugar

1 tsp (5 ml) cocoa powder

1/2 cup (125 ml) low sodium chicken or vegetable stock

1/2 cup (125 ml) cream (optional)

QUESADILLAS

10-7 inch (18 cm) flour tortillas /1 package

3 cups (750 ml) mozzarella, grated

2 cups (500 ml) cooked chicken, shredded (about 3 breasts)

1 cup (250 ml) cooked corn

1/2 cup (125 ml) cilantro, chopped

1/4 cup (60 ml) vegetable oil

1 cup (250 ml) sour cream

juice of 1/2 lime

2 limes, halved

METHOD

Place the pumpkin seeds and peanuts on a baking sheet and bake at 350°F (180°C) until toasted and golden, about 10 minutes. Cool slightly.

Heat 2 tbsp (30 ml) olive oil in a pan, add the onion and garlic and sauté until softened.

Put the cooled, toasted seeds, nuts, onions, and garlic in a food processor and pulse until combined.

Add the canned chilies, chipotle in adobo, cinnamon, chili powder, cumin, salt, maple syrup, cocoa powder and chicken stock; process until smooth, scraping down the sides of the bowl once.

Pour the mixture in a heavy bottomed pot and add cream.

Bring to a boil and then down to a simmer for 5 minutes.

Cool and refrigerate until needed.

Assemble the quesadilla by putting some cheese, chicken, corn, cilantro and about 2 tbsp (30 ml) of the mole sauce on one half of a tortilla. Fold it over and press firmly on seam. Assemble all of the tortillas and stack on a platter, cover tightly with plastic wrap and refrigerate until ready to grill. These can be assembled the day before you want to serve them.

Heat the grill to medium.

Brush the quesadillas with the vegetable oil and grill until the cheese is melted and you have golden brown grill marks.

Mix together the sour cream and lime juice.

Grill the lime halves alongside the quesadillas and squeeze them on top as you serve.

Garnish with some fresh cilantro and serve with the sour cream thinned with lime juice.

Serve these with any kind of fresh salsa, our Tomatillo Salsa on Page 33 would be perfect.

*Canned chipotle in adobo are smoked jalapeno peppers in a spicy tomato sauce. They are readily available at specialty stores and locally at Ellison's. Take them out of the can and keep them in a small container in the freezer as you will only use a small amount per recipe.

**Canned green chilies can be found in the Mexican section of your grocery store.

LAYERED BEAN DIP

This is a great starter if your group includes a large number of ravenous teenagers and/or people who have spent the day riding their bikes up and down our local hills (our dinners almost always include both). These people need to be fed something quickly or they'll start gnawing on your furniture. With or without your own homemade chips, this speedy and simple (make ahead) dip is always a hit.

- SERVES ABOUT 6 -

INGREDIENTS

1 can (398 ml) refried beans or 1 can (398 ml) veggie chili
2 ripe avocadoes
juice of 1 lemon
1 tbsp (15 ml) tabasco sauce
1/2 cup (125 ml) sour cream
1/2 cup (125 ml) mayonnaise
1 tsp (5 ml) chili powder
1 tsp (5 ml) cumin
1 tsp (5 ml) garlic powder
1 tsp (5 ml) paprika
1 tsp (5 ml) salt
1 tsp (5 ml) pepper
3/4 cup (175 ml) cheddar, grated
3/4 cup (175 ml) mozzarella, grated
1 bunch green onions, chopped
1/4 cup (60 ml) cilantro, chopped
1/2 cup (125 ml) pitted black olives, chopped

METHOD

Spread the beans out on the bottom of a lightly greased 9x11 inch (22x27 cm) pan.

Mash together the avocado, lemon juice and Tabasco and spread it on top of the beans.

Mix together the sour cream, mayonnaise, chili powder, cumin, garlic powder, paprika, salt and pepper, and spread it over the avocado.

Sprinkle the cheese, green onion, cilantro and black olives on top.

Bake at 350°F (180°C) for about 25 minutes until the cheese is bubbly and golden.

Serve with any kind of tortilla chips. Our Homemade Whole Wheat Tortilla Chips are on Page 34.

This can be assembled a day or two ahead, just cover and refrigerate until ready to bake.

OLD SMOKY MEATBALLS

We love Kozlik's old smoky mustard and it's pretty easy to get ahold of, but these work just as well with dijon mustard and a touch of liquid smoke. Make lots of these and freeze them for a quick party snack or some great sandwiches.

- SERVES 6 -

INGREDIENTS

1 lb (500 g) lean (not extra lean) ground beef

2 cloves garlic, minced

2 tbsp (30 ml) Kozlik's old smoky mustard or 2 tbsp (30 ml) dijon mustard and a dash (1 ml) liquid smoke

1/2 cup (125 ml) pecorino or parmesan cheese, grated

2 tsp (10 ml) tabasco sauce

1/4 cup (60 ml) oil packed sun-dried tomatoes, minced

1/4 cup (60 ml) parsley, basil or chives, finely chopped

1 tsp (5 ml) black pepper, freshly ground

1 tsp (5 ml) salt

2 tbsp (30 ml) olive oil for sautéing

METHOD

Mix all ingredients together and roll into bite-sized balls. About 1 tbsp (15 ml) per ball.

Sauté the meatballs in a nonstick pan with a little olive oil over medium heat for about 15 minutes.

Roll them around while sautéing, as they tend to brown quickly.

Serve them right away or keep warm, covered in a low oven.

You could brown them first and finish cooking them in a 350°F (180°C) oven for 15 minutes just before serving.

Use them with your favourite dipping sauce for a cocktail nibble or make them bigger and serve them on a crusty roll with melted mozzarella cheese and tomato sauce for a delicious meatball sandwich.

GOAT CHEESE AND SUN-DRIED TOMATO TERRINE

In our little group of friends we all make this a bit differently and you'll probably add your own twist too. If you keep a few of those little logs of soft goat cheese in the fridge most of the other ingredients are usually on hand in our kitchens. This can truly be whipped up in minutes and, with a loaf of fresh bread, it's always a favourite. We have Christina, our dearest friend, busy mom, teacher and food lover to thank for this. Nobody puts fantastic healthy food on the table faster than she does, and she does it everyday.

- SERVES 6 -

INGREDIENTS

8 oz (250 g) soft goat cheese
1/4 cup (60 ml) chopped oil packed sun-dried tomatoes, drained
1/2 cup (125 ml) pesto sauce, store bought or homemade
1/2 cup (125 ml) fresh parsley, chopped
1/2 cup (125 ml) fresh basil, chopped
1 tsp (5 ml) pepper, freshly ground
2 tbsp (30 ml) balsamic crema or balsamic vinegar
2 tbsp (30 ml) extra virgin olive oil
2 tbsp (30 ml) pine nuts, toasted
1/2 cup (125 ml) pitted calamata olives
1/2 cup (125 ml) caperberries*

METHOD

Beat the goat cheese until it's a little fluffy and smooth. You can do this with a bowl and wooden spoon or a mixer.

Spread half of the cheese on the serving plate then cover with the sun- dried tomatoes then the pesto and half of the herbs.

Spread the rest of the cheese on top.

Cover tightly with plastic wrap and press down gently to compress the layers a bit. Refrigerate until just before serving.

When you're ready to serve, sprinkle with remaining herbs and pepper. Drizzle with the balsamic crema and the olive oil. Scatter the pine nuts on top and put the olives and caperberries around it.

You can assemble this right on a serving platter or in a small 6 inch (15 cm) removable bottomed tart pan. Just line the tart pan with plastic wrap and assemble it so that the bottom becomes the top when you invert it on to your serving plate.

We like to serve this with the Potato Rosemary Foccacia on Page 19 or Marie's Rosemary Nut Crackers recipes on Page 22.
*Caperberries are the oblong shaped fruit of the caper plant. They are about the size of a grape and have a lemony taste that is a little milder than the more common caper buds. We adore them and always pick up a few jars when we visit the fabulous Ferraro Foods in Trail or Rossland.

DRY RUBBED ORANGE AND HONEY GLAZED RIBLETS

These little morsels are spicy, sweet and tender and they make a wonderful beginning to any casual dinner party. Ask your butcher to cut the rack of ribs in half lengthwise in order to create the riblets.

- SERVES ABOUT 6 -

INGREDIENTS

1 rack baby back ribs approximately 1.25 kg (cut in half lengthwise, then into individual riblets)

THE RUB

1 tbsp (15 ml) brown sugar
1 tsp (5 ml) coarse salt
1 tsp (5 ml) black pepper, freshly ground
1 tsp (5 ml) fennel seeds
1 tsp (5 ml) coriander seeds
1 tsp (5 ml) yellow mustard seeds
1 tsp (5 ml) smoked paprika
1 tbsp (15 ml) garlic, minced
1 tbsp (15 ml) ginger, minced
1 tbsp (15 ml) olive oil
zest of 1 orange

GLAZE

1/2 cup (125 ml) honey
1/2 cup (125 ml) dry sherry
1/2 cup (125 ml) orange juice

METHOD

Put the brown sugar, coarse salt, black pepper, fennel, coriander and mustard seeds into a spice grinder, and grind until fairly fine. You could also use your coffee grinder just don't forget to clean it afterward. A mortar and pestle would be even better.

Mix the ground spice mixture together with the smoked paprika, garlic, ginger, olive oil and orange zest. Rub the spices well into the meat, cover and refrigerate for at least a couple of hours or overnight.

Preheat the oven to 300°F (140°C). Place the ribs in a shallow 9x11 inch (22x27 cm) baking pan. Cover tightly with foil and bake for an hour.

Mix the glaze ingredients together in a small saucepan and simmer for a few minutes.

Remove ribs from oven. Take off foil, drain off excess fat and pour the glaze over, tossing with tongs to coat.

Cook for another 45 minutes at 350°F (180°C) without the cover, frequently tossing to glaze the ribs.

Serve on a platter with lots of napkins handy.

Grind up more of the spices than you need for this recipe and keep it in a small jar; try it on some lamb chops or chicken. You can add so much flavour quickly and easily to your food by experimenting with your spices. Create your own signature dry rub.

SWEET AND SALTY CHICKEN WINGS

One of the tastiest and easiest things you can do with a chicken wing. These are great on the barbeque because there's not much sugar in the marinade so the wings don't scorch easily (and husbands don't get in trouble for burning them). Hmmm...maybe they could start making the marinade themselves too.

- SERVES 6 -

INGREDIENTS

3 1/2 lbs approximately (1.75 kg) whole chicken wings
1/4 cup (60 ml) soy sauce
1/2 cup (125 ml) fresh lime juice and zest of 2 limes (no substitutions)
1 tbsp (15 ml) honey
1 tsp (5 ml) crushed cumin seeds or 1 tsp (5 ml) ground cumin
1 tsp (5 ml) hot spanish paprika (pimenton)*
4 cloves garlic, minced
1 tsp (5 ml) pepper, freshly ground
1 tbsp (15 ml) coarse salt
2 limes, quartered for garnish

METHOD

Rinse the chicken and cut off the wing tips, pat dry, put in a large freezer bag or a container with a tight fitting lid.
Whisk up all remaining ingredients except salt and limes.
Pour marinade over the wings.
Seal and shake up to distribute marinade. Put in the fridge for at least 6 hours, preferably overnight.
Take the wings out of the marinade and pat them dry a little before sprinkling them all over with the salt.
Reserve the marinade and boil it over medium heat to reduce it a bit (about 5 minutes).
Cook the wings on a low barbeque or in a 375°F (190°C) oven for about 35 minutes, brushing them with the reduced marinade a couple of times.
Serve with wedges of fresh lime and something cold and delicious to drink. These taste better when you're wearing your bathing suit and you can use the lake as a finger bowl.

*Spanish paprika or "pimenton" is paprika from the La Vera region in Spain where the peppers are harvested and smoke dried in an age-old traditional method. There are three kinds with varying degrees of heat. We like the hot, but start with a little at first and soon you too will love its intriguing, deep flavour. It comes in a small tin and it keeps for about two years.

You can find it locally at Ellison's Market and Culinary Conspiracy.

TOMATILLO SALSA

Tomatillo means "little tomato" in Mexico so we like to combine them with sweet little cherry tomatoes for this tart, fresh tasting salsa.

- SERVES 6 -

INGREDIENTS

4 tomatillos, husks removed, rinsed and diced*
1 pint container (475 ml) cherry or grape tomatoes, diced
1/2 medium white onion, diced
2 cloves garlic, minced
1/2 bunch cilantro, chopped
1 small jalapeno pepper, seeded and finely diced
1 tsp (5 ml) salt
juice of 1/2 to 1 whole lime (depending on the juiciness of the lime and your taste)
2 tbsp (30 ml) olive oil

METHOD

Mix everything together in a bowl and taste for seasoning.
Cover and refrigerate until needed. You should make it at least an hour ahead to let the flavours develop.

*Tomatillos are quite readily available these days. Look for firm, bright green fruit and a fresh look to the papery husk that surrounds them. Once the husk is removed they have a sticky coating that should be rinsed off before you use them.

Try this with our Whole Wheat Tortillas Chips on Page 34.

WHOLE WHEAT TORTILLA CHIPS

Making your own chips may seem ridiculous, but just try it once. There is nothing like a fresh chip and all of your lucky friends will agree.

- SERVES 6 TO 10 -

INGREDIENTS

1 package thin 10 inch whole wheat tortillas
2 cups (500 ml) vegetable oil
sea salt or coarse kosher salt to taste

METHOD

Prepare a baking sheet lined with a couple of sheets of paper towel close to your stovetop (but not too close). Have a pair of tongs, a large scoop and some salt handy.

Cut tortillas into wedges. Each tortilla will make 16 chips.

Heat the oil in a heavy bottomed pot with high sides until hot but not smoking (test it with piece of tortilla; it should float right up to the top and start to turn golden pretty quickly).

Drop a handful of chips into the hot oil (carefully) and use your tongs to wiggle them around. When they are nicely browned, remove them with your scoop and sprinkle them with a little salt.

Continue until all the chips are done. You may need to adjust your heat periodically.

The chips are best served the day they're made, but day old chips can be warmed up in the oven for a few minutes.

SALADS

WARM GOAT CHEESE SALAD WITH SHALLOT VINAIGRETTE

What's better than warm cheese on a bed of fresh greens...? Not much. Add a luscious sautéed shallot vinaigrette and you have a salad that's perfect for entertaining or a treat for a cozy family dinner.

- SERVES 4 -

INGREDIENTS

8 cups (2 L) mixed greens, washed and dried
2/3 cup (150 ml) dry breadcrumbs (panko)
1/4 cup (60 ml) parsley, chopped
1/2 tsp (2 ml) pepper, freshly ground
1/2 tsp (2 ml) salt
1 egg mixed with 1 tbsp (15 ml) water
6 oz (200 g) soft goat cheese
1/4 cup (60 ml) dried cherries*
1/4 cup (60 ml) pinenuts, toasted

DRESSING

2 tbsp (30 ml) olive oil
1/2 cup (125 ml) shallots, diced
1/4 cup (60 ml) white wine vinegar
2 tbsp (30 ml) maple syrup or honey
1/2 cup (125 ml) olive oil
salt and pepper to taste
1/4 cup (60 ml) vegetable oil

METHOD

Mix together the breadcrumbs, chopped parsley, pepper and salt in a small bowl.
Put the egg mixture in another small bowl.
Roll the goat cheese into small 1 tbsp (15 ml) balls. You should have 12 balls of cheese. Dip the cheese balls into the egg mixture, rolling them around to coat. Roll them in the breadcrumbs, gently pressing to adhere the crumbs to the cheese.
Cover and refrigerate for at least an hour.

Make the dressing by heating the 2 tbsp (30 ml) olive oil and sautéing the shallots until softened and golden brown. Add the vinegar and maple syrup or honey and reduce for a minute or two.
Remove from the heat and whisk in the 1/2 cup (125 ml) olive oil. Season to taste with salt and pepper.

Heat the vegetable oil in a sauté pan over medium high heat until hot but not smoking. Add the goat cheese balls and brown them quickly on all sides.
Toss the dressing lightly with the greens and divide them between 4 plates.
Place 3 balls of cheese on each salad and sprinkle the dried cherries and toasted pine nuts on top.
Drizzle a little more dressing on the salad.
Serve right away.

*Dried cranberries are a good substitute for the cherries.

HOUSE SALAD

Every once in a while we create an easy salad made out of things we have on hand. If it turns into a hit with the family, it can become our house salad for months. We don't eat this every night...but at least once a week.

- SERVES 4 -

INGREDIENTS

1 head red leaf lettuce, or 6 cups spring greens
1 beet, peeled and grated
1/2 cup (125 ml) feta, crumbled
1/2 cup (125 ml) pumpkin seeds, toasted
1/2 cup (125 ml) cherry tomatoes, quartered
1/2 cup (125 ml) fresh dill

DRESSING

1/4 cup (60 ml) balsamic crema*
1/4 cup (60 ml) extra virgin olive oil
1 tbsp (15 ml) fresh dill, chopped
1 tsp (5 ml) salt
1 tsp (5 ml) pepper

METHOD

Put the greens in salad bowl, or on individual plates.
Place the grated beets, feta, pumpkin seeds, tomatoes and chopped fresh dill on top of the greens.
Make the dressing by combining the balsamic crema, olive oil, dill, salt and pepper.
Drizzle over the salad and give it a little toss.

*Available at the Railway Station Specialty Meats and Deli.

For a change from plain toasted pumpkin seeds try this:

Melt 1 tbsp (15 ml) butter and add 1 tsp (5 ml) dill, 1/2 tsp (2 ml) cumin, 1/2 tsp (2 ml) paprika, 1/2 tsp (2 ml) salt and 1/2 tsp (2 ml) sugar. Pour the spiced butter over 1 cup (250 ml) of pumpkin seeds, toss together and roast in the oven at 350°F(180°C) for 15 minutes. You'll have seeds left over for another salad or two.

BEEF TENDERLOIN SALAD WITH ROASTED BEETS, SHALLOTS, ASPARAGUS AND HORSERADISH CREAM

Get out a big beautiful platter and serve this main course salad to some lucky pals for a casual feast. Roast the vegetables ahead and keep them at room temperature for an easy, last minute flinging together. Try to find some nice, peppery greens, like arugula for this.

- SERVES 6 TO 8 -

HORSERADISH CREAM

3/4 cup (175 ml) sour cream
1/4 cup (60 ml) whipping cream
2 tbsp (30 ml) prepared horseradish
juice of 1 lemon
1/2 tsp (2 ml) salt
1/2 tsp (2 ml) pepper

INGREDIENTS

1 1/2 lbs (750 g) baby beets scrubbed and trimmed
8 medium sized shallots, peeled and left whole
1/4 cup (60 ml) balsamic vinegar
1/4 cup (60 ml) olive oil
1 tsp (5 ml) salt
1 tsp (5 ml) pepper, freshly ground
one 3 1/2 lb (1.75 kg) beef tenderloin fillet
2 tbsp (30 ml) fresh rosemary, chopped
1 tbsp (15 ml) mustard powder
2 tsp (10 ml) coarse salt
2 tsp (10 ml) freshly ground pepper
1 bunch asparagus, trimmed
10 cups (2.5 L) greens (arugula)
juice of 1 lemon
2 tbsp (30 ml) olive oil
salt and pepper
1/2 cup (125 ml) shaved pecorino romano cheese

METHOD

Make the horseradish cream by combining sour cream, whipping cream, horseradish, lemon juice, salt and pepper.

Toss the beets and shallots with the balsamic vinegar, olive oil, salt and pepper and place on a baking pan. Cover with foil and bake in a 350°F (180°C) oven until tender, about 40 minutes.

Trim the beef of any bits of fat. Rub the meat all over with the rosemary, mustard, salt and pepper.

Sear the beef in a hot ovenproof pan with a little olive oil until it's well browned on all sides. Place it in a 350°F (180°C) oven and roast for about 20 minutes for medium rare, or until desired doneness.

Take it out and let it rest, covered for at least 10 minutes.

Roll the asparagus in a little olive oil, salt and pepper and roast on a separate sheet pan at 350°F (180°C) for about 20 minutes until tender.

Assemble the salad. Toss the greens with a little lemon juice and olive oil and arrange on a large platter.

Slice the beef very thinly and arrange on top of the greens.

Scatter the beets, shallots and asparagus all over. Dot with some of the horseradish cream and sprinkle with the shaved cheese.

Serve the remaining dressing on the side.

We often serve this with lots of crusty buns, especially when the crowd includes our sandwich loving teenagers.

GERI'S BUTTER LETTUCE, RADICCHIO AND GREEN GODDESS SALAD

This is a big salad but Geri has a big family and this is what she makes when everybody comes home for dinner. We love the simplicity of this salad, the contrast between the sweet butter lettuce and the bite of the radicchio with the creamy dressing.

- SERVES 8 TO 10 -

INGREDIENTS

2 heads butter lettuce, about 12 cups (3 L)
1 small head radicchio

DRESSING

1/2 cup (125 ml) mayonnaise
1/2 cup (125 ml) sour cream
1 tbsp (15 ml) anchovy paste or 3 anchovies, drained
1 tbsp (15 ml) lime juice
2 tbsp (30 ml) white wine vinegar
2 tsp (10 ml) finely chopped fresh tarragon
or 1 tsp (5 ml) dried
2 tbsp (30 ml) chopped chives or tops of green onions
1/4 cup (60 ml) chopped parsley
1/2 cup (125 ml) spinach leaves packed
pinch (1 ml) sea salt
pinch (1 ml) black pepper
1 tbsp (15 ml) parsley, chopped

METHOD

Separate the leaves of the butter lettuce and radicchio, wash and dry well. Wrap in paper towel, put in a plastic bag and refrigerate for at least an hour or until ready to use.
Combine all dressing ingredients in a blender or food processor.
Process until smooth.
Remove the lettuce and radicchio from the fridge just before serving. Place the lettuce and radicchio in a big salad bowl. Pour some of the dressing over and toss to coat. (Depending on your taste you may not need all the dressing.)
Season with salt and pepper and sprinkle with chopped parsley.

Use as a dip for any kind of crudite or as a dressing for some blanched and chilled cauliflower. Almost any vegetable would benefit from this creamy herby deliciousness.

QUINOA WITH SAFFRON, FIGS AND PISTACHIOS

This salad comes from Caren McSherry, owner of The Gourmet Warehouse and author of some of our favourite cookbooks. This is our adaptation of her bold and flavourful Middle Eastern Couscous Salad. Caren has been a kind and enthusiastic supporter of Whitewater Cooks and we owe her a big thank you. Her beautiful store, on Hastings Street in Vancouver, always tops the list of our places to go when we get to the big city. It's pure nirvana for foodies like us, so make sure to check it out.

- SERVES 8 TO 10 -

INGREDIENTS

1/2 cup (125 ml) sweet port
1 cup (250 ml) black mission figs, quartered
1/4 cup (60 ml) butter
1 large white onion, diced
2 cloves garlic, minced
1/2 jalapeno pepper, seeded and finely diced
1 tsp (5 ml) cinnamon
2 tsp (10 ml) ground cumin
1 tsp (5 ml) cardamom
1 tsp (5 ml) saffron threads*
4 cups (1 L) low sodium chicken stock
3 cups (750 ml) quinoa, rinsed well
2 large red peppers, diced
2 oranges, peeled and segmented
1/2 cup (125 ml) parsley, chopped
1/2 cup (125 ml) cilantro, chopped
1/2 cup (125 ml) fresh mint, chopped
1 tsp (5 ml) sea salt
1 tsp (5 ml) black pepper
1 cup (250 ml) pistachio nuts, chopped**
sprigs of mint for garnish

METHOD

Heat the port in a little pot and add figs. Let simmer for about 5 minutes. Set aside.

Melt the butter in a large frying pan and add the onion, garlic and jalapeno. Sauté until the onion is golden brown. Add cinnamon, cumin and cardamom, cook for another minute.

Put the quinoa in a pot and add the chicken stock and saffron. Bring to a boil over medium heat, turn down to simmer and cook for about 15 minutes. The quinoa should be opened up to reveal a little spiral and be tender to chew.

Drain excess water through a fine mesh strainer.

Spread the quinoa out on a cookie sheet to cool.

Place cooled quinoa in a large bowl and stir in the onion spice mixture, red peppers, oranges, figs, parsley, cilantro, mint, salt and pepper.

Garnish with pistachios and big sprigs of mint.

*Saffron comes in small handy portions at the Kootenay Co-op.
**Shelled pistachio nuts can be found in the bulk section of most major grocery stores.

RIVER WRAPS

One of the best things to do on a hot, sunny Kootenay day is to head to the Slocan River and watch the clear, blue water roll by from a sandy beach. We've spent many days like this and these healthy, delicious wraps are just what we like to have packed in the cooler.

- MAKES 6 WRAPS -

INGREDIENTS

2 tbsp (30 ml) vegetable oil
2 medium onions, sliced
1/4 cup (60 ml) barbeque sauce
1 tsp (5 ml) pepper
2 cups (500 ml) broccoli
2 cups (500 ml) cauliflower
1 cup (250 ml) carrot, grated about 1 large
1 cup (250 ml) red cabbage, grated about 1/4 head
3 dill pickles, slivered
1/3 cup (75 ml) mayonnaise
1 tsp (5 ml) chile in adobo (optional)
1 head leafy green lettuce, washed and dried
6-10 inch (25 cm) whole wheat tortillas

METHOD

Heat the vegetable oil in a frying pan, add the onions and sauté for about 10 minutes until soft and beginning to colour. Add the barbeque sauce and continue cooking until the sauce is absorbed and the onions are just beginning to stick to the pan. Add pepper. Set aside to cool.

Break up the broccoli and cauliflower into small pieces and blanch it in boiling water for a couple of minutes.

Plunge it into a bowl of cold water. Drain well and dry.

Mix together the mayonnaise with the chili in adobo in a small bowl.

Put all your prepped ingredients in bowls. Lay out a 10 inch (25 cm) piece of plastic wrap on your counter.

Toast one tortilla in a lightly oiled frying pan for a minute or two on each side. Let it cool slightly and lay it on the plastic wrap.

Assemble the wrap by spreading the tortilla with some of the mayonnaise and the onion mixture. Add a line of broccoli and cauliflower, a line of pickles, a line of grated carrot and red cabbage and top with lettuce.

Roll up the tortilla as tightly as you can, folding up the ends of the plastic wrap and making a nice tight roll. Don't worry about any tears in the tortilla, just carry on. You can always eat your mistakes later.

Proceed with the rest of the wraps.

We like to toast the tortillas to bring out the nutty, whole wheat flavour but you don't have to. If you do, be careful not to make them too crisp or you'll have trouble rolling them up neatly.These wraps will last refrigerated for a couple of days.

COOL SESAME MISO NOODLE SALAD

We've dragged this inexpensive, easy to make and tasty salad around to more pot lucks and beach barbeques than you could shake a stick at. Everybody loves it, including the kids.

- SERVES 8 TO 10 -

INGREDIENTS

1 package (500 g) angel hair pasta

2 tbsp (30 ml) fresh ginger, grated and chopped

2 garlic cloves, crushed

1 tbsp (15 ml) miso paste

1/2 cup (125 ml) rice wine vinegar

1/4 cup (60 ml) soy sauce or tamari

1/4 cup (60 ml) sesame oil

1 tsp (5 ml) curry powder

1 tbsp (15 ml) sweet chili sauce

juice of 2 limes

1/2 cup (125 ml) vegetable oil

1 bunch green onions, chopped diagonally

1 bunch cilantro, chopped

1 cup (250 ml) toasted peanuts, chopped

METHOD

Cook noodles until al dente, rinse in cold water and drain well.

Combine ginger, garlic, miso, rice vinegar, soy sauce, sesame oil, curry powder, sweet chili sauce and lime juice in medium bowl and mix well.

Add oil in a slow steady stream until combined.

Add cooled noodles to the bowl with the dressing and toss well.

Place in pretty serving bowl or platter and garnish with green onions, cilantro and peanuts.

Our friend Mia served big bowls of these fabulous chilled noodles at her sister's outdoor wedding accompanied by Cedar Planked Salmon, which can be found on Page 108. It was a match made in heaven!

KAREN'S ROASTED POTATO AND FRESH MINT SALAD

Sometimes the simplest recipes are the best, and this one is all about the cooking technique of the potatoes. It's great right out of the oven, or at room temperature. Something about the crunchiness of the sea salt and the freshness of the mint makes this potato salad a winner.

- SERVES 6 TO 8 -

INGREDIENTS

2 lbs (about 1 kg) red nugget potatoes (the smaller the better)
3/4 cup (175 ml) olive oil
1 tbsp (15 ml) garlic, minced
1 cup (250 ml) fresh mint, chopped
2 tbsp (30 ml) chunky sea salt

METHOD

Preheat oven to 400°F (200°C).
Pierce potatoes with a small fork or skewer and place on a dry sheet pan.
Roast in oven until soft on the inside and crispy on the outside, about 30 minutes.
Remove from oven.
Cut them in half and place in a serving bowl or deep platter.
Combine olive oil, garlic and mint and pour over potatoes. Toss until coated.
Sprinkle generously with sea salt.

These potatoes go well with anything. Grilled lamb chops and some beautiful, sliced, just picked tomatoes would be a simple yet divine combination.

PETRA'S PAELLA SALAD

This salad is based on the classic Spanish dish paella. A great make ahead dish as the saffron infused rice gets even better when chilled, not to mention how smug you'll be to have this beautiful salad all ready to go the next day. This is another outstanding recipe from Petra, a wonderful home cook and a dear, helpful pal.

- SERVES 10 TO 12 -

DRESSING

2 tbsp (30 ml) fresh lemon juice
2 tbsp (30 ml) sun-dried tomatoes, chopped
2 cloves garlic, minced
2 tbsp (30 ml) red wine vinegar
1 tsp (5 ml) salt
1 tsp (5 ml) pepper
1 cup (250 ml) olive oil

INGREDIENTS

2 1/2 cups (625 ml) low sodium chicken broth
1 cup (250 ml) clam nectar
1 cup (250 ml) dry white wine
1 tsp (5 ml) saffron threads
1 tbsp (15 ml) olive oil
1 large onion, diced
2 garlic cloves, minced
1 jalapeno pepper, seeded and chopped finely
2 red peppers, diced
2 yellow peppers, diced
2 hot italian sausages (optional) sliced diagonally into thick slices
2 cups (500 ml) uncooked long grained white rice
1 tsp (5 ml) paprika
1 tsp (5 ml) thyme
1 tsp (5 ml) oregano
4 medium tomatoes, diced
4 green onions, thinly sliced
1 1/2 cups (375 ml) peas, thawed
3/4 cup (175 ml) fresh cilantro, chopped
1 bag (454 ml) prawns, peeled and cooked
salt and pepper to taste

METHOD

Combine lemon juice, sun-dried tomatoes, garlic, vinegar, salt and pepper and mix well. Add olive oil in steady stream until blended. Make this in a food processor if you have one.

Pour broth, clam nectar, and wine into large bowl. Stir in saffron and leave to steep.

Heat oil in a large saucepan over medium heat.

Add onion, garlic, jalapenos, red and yellow peppers and sausages. Stir often until sausages are lightly browned, 5 to 6 minutes.

Stir in rice, paprika, thyme and oregano. Pour in the saffron mixture. Increase heat to high and bring mixture to a boil, stirring often. Cover and reduce heat to medium low. Simmer, stirring occasionally until rice is tender and liquid has been absorbed, 25 to 30 minutes.

Spread out on a large baking sheet with shallow sides, to cool the rice quickly.

Refrigerate the rice mixture uncovered, stirring occasionally until rice is cool, about 20 minutes.

Put the rice into a large bowl and add the tomatoes, green onions, peas, and cilantro and toss well.

Pour in the salad dressing, add the prawns and mix just to combine.

Taste and season with salt and pepper if necessary.

If you feel like firing up the barbeque try grilling the sausages and the prawns and adding them after the dressing.

BLUE CHEESE, BOSC PEAR AND PECAN SALAD

This is our twist on an oldie that we think is a real goodie. You need a nice, large, firm head of iceberg lettuce for this.

- SERVES 4 -

DRESSING

1/2 cup (125 ml) yogurt
1/2 cup (125 ml) mayonnaise
2 oz (60 g) blue cheese, crumbled (your favourite kind)
1 tbsp (15 ml) lemon juice
1/2 tsp (2 ml) salt
1/2 tsp (2 ml) pepper

INGREDIENTS

1 head iceberg lettuce
1 tbsp (15 ml) butter
1 cup (250 ml) pecans
1 tbsp (15 ml) maple syrup
1 bosc pear
1 tbsp (15 ml) lemon juice
2 oz (60 g) blue cheese
1/2 cup (125 ml) flat leafed parsley

METHOD

Make the dressing in a small bowl by mixing together the yogurt, mayonnaise, blue cheese, lemon juice, salt and pepper.

Cut the lettuce into 4 wedges and soak them in a bowl of ice water for 30 minutes. Drain and shake off as much water as you can just before serving, taking care not to break up the wedge.
Melt the butter in a skillet and toast the pecans for a couple of minutes, adding the maple syrup and stirring until glazed. Set aside to cool.
Core the pear and cut into 8 wedges, squeeze 1 tbsp (15 ml) lemon juice over them to prevent discolouring.
Assemble the salad on individual serving plates by placing one piece of drained lettuce and 2 wedges of pear on each plate, pouring some of the dressing over top and sprinkling with the glazed pecans. Finish it by slicing the blue cheese and placing it on each plate. Sprinkle with the chopped parsley.

Soaking the lettuce in ice water is an important step. Your lettuce will be crisp and crunchy which is what you want for this simple yet decadent salad. This salad is also great made with romaine hearts.

WARM RED CABBAGE SALAD WITH PANCETTA AND GOAT CHEESE

Affectionately named "the greasy salad", it isn't really. This totally addictive salad is smoky and smooth with a nice bite from the radicchio. It comes from fond memories of dining in a little, long gone Italian restaurant in West Vancouver. They made a salad that was something like this and we couldn't get enough of it.

- SERVES 6 -

INGREDIENTS

1 tsp (5 ml) olive oil

1 cup (250 g) pancetta, or bacon, diced

1/2 head of red cabbage, shredded finely, like coleslaw

1 small head of radicchio, thinly sliced

1/2 red onion, thinly sliced

1/2 cup (125 ml) olive oil

1/4 cup (60 ml) red wine vinegar

2 cups (500 ml) arugula

1 cup (250 ml) fresh basil, julienned

4 oz (125 g) soft goat cheese, crumbled

1/2 cup (125 ml) pine nuts, toasted

METHOD

Heat 1 tsp (5 ml) oil in large wok or pan over medium high heat.

Add pancetta and sauté until crispy and the juices have run out, about 10 minutes.

Add cabbage, radicchio and red onion and cook for another about 10 minutes, until slightly wilted and soft.

Turn off heat and add the remaining olive oil and vinegar and toss to coat. The oil and vinegar will be absorbed into the hot cabbage.

Add the arugula, basil, goat cheese and pine nuts and give it a gentle toss.

Transfer to individual plates and serve right out of the hot pan.

This salad would cozy up divinely with the Fennel Infused Roast Pork Loin on Page 130.

ARUGULA SALAD WITH MANCHEGO CHEESE, TOASTED HAZELNUTS AND QUINCE DRESSING

This comes from Barb Gosney, our pal and domestic goddess who makes her own quince jelly and grows vast amounts of arugula in her garden. All of these assertive flavours meld together to give this salad a typical Spanish flavour.

- SERVES 4 -

QUINCE DRESSING

1/4 cup (60 ml) quince jelly*
2 tbsp (30 ml) red wine vinegar
1 tsp (5 ml) lemon juice, fresh
1 tsp (5 ml) salt
1 tsp (5 ml) black pepper
2 tbsp (30 ml) olive or hazelnut oil

INGREDIENTS

6 cups (1.5 L) arugula, stems removed
4 oz (125 g) manchego cheese, shaved**
1/2 cup (125 g) hazelnuts, toasted and roughly chopped

METHOD

Put the quince jelly, vinegar, lemon juice, salt and pepper in a mixing bowl and mix well.
Add the oil and whisk until combined.
Toss the arugula with the dressing, most of the shaved cheese and hazelnuts.
Sprinkle the remaining cheese and nuts on top of the salad.

*Quince jelly can be found at Culinary Conspiracy.
**Manchego is Spain's most famous cheese export. It's made from sheep's milk and has a firm, somewhat crumbly texture and a delicious intense flavour. It's available at the Railway Station Specialty Meats and Deli.

To toast the hazelnuts, place nuts on a baking tray and roast in a 350° F (180°C) oven until golden, about 15 minutes. Roll nuts between a tea towel until skins fall off.

YUKON GOLD POTATO AND YAM SALAD

A sweet and tangy variation on everyone's favourite picnic salad.

- SERVES 6 -

INGREDIENTS

1 lb (500 g) yams, peeled and chopped into 1 inch (2.5 cm) cubes

1 tbsp (15 ml) vegetable oil

1 lb (500 g) yukon gold potatoes, peeled and chopped into 1 inch (2.5 ml) cubes

1 medium white onion, finely chopped

6 stalks celery, finely chopped

1 cup (250 ml) fresh dill

2 tbsp (30 ml) capers, drained

DRESSING

1/4 cup (60 ml) dijon mustard

juice and zest of 1 lemon

1/4 cup (60 ml) apple cider vinegar

2 tbsp (30 ml) honey

1 tsp (5 ml) white pepper

2 tsp (10 ml) salt

3/4 cup (175 ml) olive oil

METHOD

Preheat oven to 375°F (190°C).

Toss yam cubes with 1 tbsp (15 ml) vegetable oil and spread out on a large baking sheet. Roast in the oven, stirring occasionally until tender, about 30 minutes. Cool completely.

Bring the potatoes to a boil in a pot of lightly salted water. Cook covered for about 20 minutes until the potatoes are just tender. Drain well then spread the potatoes out on a large baking sheet so that they cool more quickly.

Combine onion, celery, dill and capers in a bowl big enough to hold the yams and potatoes.

Make the dressing by combining mustard, lemon juice and zest, apple cider vinegar, honey, pepper and salt with a whisk. Add olive oil in a steady stream until emulsified.

Toss the cooled yams and potatoes with the onions, celery, dill and capers.

Pour the dressing over the salad and toss gently to combine.

Store the salad at room temperature if serving within a few hours.

Because it has no mayonnaise or eggs, this is a great potato salad to bring along when you can't fit another thing into the cooler or refrigeration is not available.

ROASTED VEGETABLE SALAD

You can play around with the vegetables, by using a little more or less of whatever you have on hand, but do include the parsnips as they really enhance this earthy and satisfying salad.

- SERVES 6 TO 8 -

INGREDIENTS

1 large yam, peeled and diced in 1 inch (2.5 cm) cubes

2 large parsnips, peeled, quartered and sliced

1 fennel bulb, quartered and sliced thinly

1 red onion, chopped in 1 inch (2.5 cm) dice

2 red peppers, chopped in 1 inch (2.5 cm) dice

2 zucchini, quartered and sliced thickly

1 lb (500 g) mushrooms, quartered

1 eggplant, diced in 1 inch (2.5 cm) cubes

3 beets, peeled and quartered

1/2 cup (125 ml) olive oil

1 tsp (5 ml) salt

1 tsp (5 ml) black pepper

1 tbsp (15 ml) garlic, minced

DRESSING

1/3 cup (75 ml) balsamic vinegar

3 tbsp (45 ml) maple syrup (the real stuff)

2 tbsp (30 ml) dijon mustard (grainy is fine)

2 tsp (10 ml) garlic, minced

1 tsp (5 ml) salt

1 tsp (5 ml) black pepper

1 cup (250 ml) vegetable or olive oil

2 cups (500 ml) fresh basil, julienned

METHOD

Preheat oven to 375°F (190°C).

Prepare all vegetables, placing yams and parsnips in one bowl, beets in their own bowl and remaining veggies in another.

Whisk together olive oil, salt, pepper and 1 tbsp (15 ml) of garlic. Divide oil mixture between the three bowls of chopped veggies and toss to coat.

Put the parsnips, yams and beets on a parchment paper lined baking sheet, leaving a little border between the beets so they don't run into the other veggies. Sometimes we use the fennel fronds to create a wall between them.

Put the rest of the vegetables on another parchment paper lined baking sheet.

Roast for about 20 minutes, stirring and rotating the pans once, or until onions are just softened. Remove the fennel and onion mixture and leave the beets, yams and parsnips to roast until just tender and a little crisp (another 15-20 minutes). Cool all vegetables to room temperature.

Make the dressing by combining the balsamic vinegar, maple syrup, dijon mustard, remaining garlic, and salt and pepper in a small mixing bowl. Add the oil in a steady stream whisking until the dressing is thick and emulsified.

Toss the roasted vegetables with the dressing, adding the beets after all the other vegetables have been added.

Garnish with the fresh basil and serve it on a big oval platter or a pretty bowl.

You will probably have some dressing left over but it's delicious on almost any type of green salad.

SEARED DUCK AND ORANGE SALAD

Don't let the idea of cooking a duck breast rattle you. This is a simple preparation that takes no time at all to cook and rewards you with something a little different and utterly delectable. A romantic lunch for two or an elegant starter for four.

- SERVES 2 (OR 4) -

INGREDIENTS

4 cups (1 L) spring greens, washed and dried well

1 endive, sliced lengthwise

1 large orange, peeled and segmented

1/2 cup (125 ml) slivered almonds, toasted

2 duck breasts, boneless, skin on (about 450 g)*

DRESSING

1/2 cup (125 ml) orange juice

1 shallot, chopped

1/4 cup (60 ml) sherry wine vinegar

1/2 tsp (2 ml) chinese 5 spice powder

1 tsp (5 ml) dijon mustard

2 tsp (10 ml) soya sauce

1/2 cup (125 ml) olive oil

salt and pepper to taste

METHOD

Preheat oven to 400°F (200°C).

Make the dressing by putting the orange juice, chopped shallots and sherry vinegar in a small pot. Reduce over medium heat by half. Remove from the heat.

Stir in the chinese 5 spice, dijon, soy sauce and then add the olive oil in a stream, whisking to emulsify. Set aside.

Score the skin of the duck breasts with a very sharp knife in a crisscross pattern. Season both sides with salt and pepper.

Place the duck in a hot ovenproof sauté pan skin side down first and sear for about 4 minutes per side.

Put the duck breasts in the hot oven for 10 to 15 minutes.

Remove from the oven, cover and let them rest for about 10 minutes while you prepare the rest of your salad.

Toss the greens with some of the dressing and divide it between your plates. Place the orange slices and endive leaves on top.

Slice the fat off the duck breast and discard. Slice the duck horizontally, then cut the slices in half to create julienned pieces.

Toss the duck with the rest of the dressing and arrange it on the salad. Sprinkle with the toasted almonds and serve.

*Duck breasts can be found frozen at many grocery stores and locally at the Railway Station Specialty Meats and Deli.

SHRIMP, MANGO AND CUCUMBER SALAD

This is light, pretty and really uncomplicated. Just use the freshest ingredients you can find.

INGREDIENTS

1 lb (500 g) fresh (hand peeled if possible) shrimp
1 ripe mango, diced
1 ripe avocado, diced
1 cup (250 ml) long english cucumber, diced
1/2 medium red onion, finely diced
1 cup (250 ml) cilantro, chopped
1 small jalapeno pepper, seeded and finely diced
1/3 cup (75 ml) lime juice (about 2 limes)
1 tsp (5 ml) lime zest
2 tsp (10 ml) tabasco sauce
1 tbsp (15 ml) olive oil
salt and pepper to taste

METHOD

Place the shrimp in a colander and press down a little to remove any excess moisture.
Transfer shrimp to a large bowl.
Add all other ingredients and mix together gently.
Taste and season with salt and pepper.
Serve garnished with cilantro leaves and some lime wedges.

This salad becomes a great appetizer when served on our Wonton Crisps which can be found on Page 10 and also makes a great sandwich filling.

SOUPS and SIDES

CURRIED LAMB & LENTIL SOUP

Erin Bates, Whitewater's multi-talented kitchen manager, made this hearty soup often this past winter and everybody loved it. Erin's used to feeding large crews of hungry tree planters and this soup will satisfy any big group of friends or family.

- SERVES 10 TO 12 -

INGREDIENTS

1 1/2 cups (375 ml) whole green lentils
1 tbsp (15 ml) vegetable oil
1 lb (500 g) boneless lamb leg or shoulder, trimmed and cubed
1 tbsp (15 ml) fresh ginger, minced
1/2 tsp (2 ml) red chili flakes
1 tsp (5 ml) turmeric
6 cups (1.5 L) water
2 tbsp (30 ml) vegetable oil
1 tsp (5 ml) fenugreek*
1 tsp (5 ml) yellow mustard seeds
1 large onion, diced
8 cloves garlic, minced
2 tbsp (30 ml) fresh ginger, minced
3 large carrots, diced
1 red pepper, diced
2 tsp (10 ml) cumin
1 tsp (5 ml) coriander
1 tsp (5 ml) garam masala
2 tsp (10 ml) salt
1-28 oz (796 ml) can diced tomatoes with juice
salt and pepper to taste
1 cup (250 ml) fresh cilantro, chopped

METHOD

Rinse lentils in several changes of cold water.
Heat oil in a large heavy bottomed stockpot over medium high heat.
Add lamb, ginger, chili flakes and turmeric. Cook, stirring until meat is brown on all sides.
Add lentils and water. Cover and bring to a boil.
Reduce heat and simmer until lentils are tender, about 45 minutes.
Heat 2 tbsp (30 ml) oil in a large skillet over medium high heat.
Add fenugreek and mustard seeds and cook until they start to pop. Add onions and sauté, stirring occasionally, until they are golden brown and caramelized (at least 10 minutes).
Add garlic, ginger, carrots and red pepper. Cook a few more minutes then add cumin, coriander, garam masala and salt. Cook, stirring occasionally, for about 10 minutes or until carrots are just tender.
Add diced tomatoes, bring to a simmer, and remove from heat.
Test the lentils for tenderness and add the onion mixture. Bring soup to a gentle boil. Reduce heat to low and continue cooking for 30 to 45 minutes. Add salt and pepper to taste.
Stir in 1 cup (250 ml) cilantro just before serving.

This recipe also makes a delicious main course curry. Just reduce the water to 4 cups and serve over basmati rice with the chutney of your choice and a piece of hot Naan bread.
*Fenugreek and other spices are best purchased in small amounts and are available locally at the Kootenay Co-op.

CHICKEN TORTILLA SOUP WITH AVOCADO AND LIME

In the Fresh Tracks Café at the beautiful Whitewater Ski Resort we serve thousands of bowls of Tortilla Soup to hungry skiers and snowboarders. There are so many recipes for this classic Mexican soup, but this is our favourite.

- SERVES 8 -

INGREDIENTS

4 corn or flour tortillas cut into thin strips, about 2 inches (5 cm) long

1/2 cup (125 ml) vegetable oil

1/4 cup (60 ml) vegetable oil, divided

2 medium onions, thinly sliced

4 cloves garlic, crushed

1/2 cup (125 ml) cilantro, chopped

one 28 oz can (796 ml) tomatoes, drained

2 tbsp (30 ml) masa harina*

1 tsp (5 ml) ground cumin

4 cups (1 L) low sodium chicken stock

1 cup (250 ml) water

2 large (500 g) skinless, boneless chicken breasts, cut into bite size pieces

2 tsp (10 ml) salt

1 tsp (5 ml) pepper

1/2 cup (125 ml) cilantro, chopped

2 avocadoes, pitted, peeled and diced

1 cup (250 ml) monterey jack cheese, grated

juice of two limes

METHOD

Cut the tortillas into thin strips.

Heat 1/2 cup (125 ml) of oil over medium high heat in deep sided frying pan.

Fry tortilla strips a few at a time until crispy and golden brown, about 3 minutes.

Remove with a slotted spoon and drain on paper towels. Set aside.

Heat 2 tbsp (30 ml) of the oil over medium high heat in a large soup pot.

Add the onion, garlic and 1/2 cup (125 ml) of the cilantro and sauté until golden brown, about 10 minutes.

Transfer the sautéed mixture to a food processor or blender and add the tomatoes. Process until smooth.

Heat another 2 tbsp (30 ml) of the oil in the soup pot over medium high heat. Add the tomato mixture, masa harina and cumin, and cook, stirring frequently until thickened, about 10 minutes.

Add chicken stock and water, bring to a simmer.

Add the chicken and cook for about 10 minutes until chicken is fully cooked.

Season with salt and pepper.

Ladle the soup into bowls and garnish with cilantro, avocado, cheese, fresh lime juice and tortillas.

*Masa harina is flour made from corn treated with lime and used in Mexican cooking for tortillas and tamales. It's sold at Ellison's Market.

BEEF, LEEK AND POT BARLEY SOUP

A soothing pot of hearty, nourishing deliciousness. Just the thing to have simmering away on the stove for a chilly fall or winter afternoon.

- SERVES 10 -

INGREDIENTS

1 tbsp (15 ml) vegetable oil

1 tsp (5 ml) salt

1/2 tsp (2 ml) pepper

4 meaty beef short ribs, bone in (about 1 kg)

2 cloves garlic, minced

2 large leeks, the white and some of the green, diced

5 stalks celery, diced

2 small or 1 large carrot, peeled and diced

1 medium onion, diced

4 cups (1 L) low sodium beef broth

4 cups (1 L) water

1 cup (250 ml) red wine

1-28 oz (796 ml) can diced tomatoes

1 tbsp (15 ml) fresh thyme, chopped or 1 tsp (5 ml) dried

1 bay leaf

3/4 cup (175 ml) pot barley

1 tbsp (15 ml) balsamic vinegar

1/4 cup (60 ml) fresh parsley, chopped

salt and pepper to taste

METHOD

Heat oil in a large heavy bottomed soup pot.

Season the meat with salt and pepper, add it to the pot and brown it well on all sides.

Add the garlic, leeks, celery, carrot and onion. Sauté while stirring until the vegetables are softened (about 5 minutes)

Add the beef broth, water, red wine, tomatoes, thyme and bay leaf. Bring the soup to a simmer, then turn the heat way down and partially cover the pot with a lid.

Simmer for an hour before adding the barley, then simmer for 1/2 hour to 3/4 of an hour more until the barley is tender and the meat is falling off the bone.

Remove the meat with a slotted spoon, dice it, discarding the bones and fat. Add the meat back to the soup.

Add the balsamic vinegar, fresh parsley and taste for seasoning, adding more salt and pepper if it needs it.

You can swap out the short ribs for one lb (500 g) of good stewing beef if you want, but we love the rich flavour that the meat on the bone gives to this soup.

SHRIMP BISQUE

When you want to feel like you're in Paris, but you're not, make this creamy, elegant bisque. A crusty baguette and a crisp green salad and voila, you're there!

- SERVES 6 TO 8 -

INGREDIENTS

1/4 cup (60 ml) butter

1 onion, diced

1 large carrot, peeled and diced

3 cloves garlic, minced

1 lb (500 g) uncooked shrimp or 1 bag (454 g)
uncooked peeled prawns, tails off

5 fresh roma tomatoes, diced

1 tbsp (15 ml) lobster paste* (optional)

2 tbsp (30 ml) tomato paste

3 cups (750 ml) fish stock, or 2 cups (500 ml)
clam nectar and 1 cup (250 ml) water

1 cup (250 ml) whipping cream

1/2 cup (125 ml) sherry

tabasco, dash (1 ml)

salt and pepper to taste

2 tbsp (30 ml) fresh lemon juice

2 tbsp (30 ml) chopped parsley

METHOD

Melt the butter in a heavy bottomed pot over medium heat.

Add the onion, carrot and garlic and sauté until slightly softened, about 5 minutes.

Add the shrimp or prawns, tomatoes, lobster and tomato pastes and stock. Stir to combine and cook until the shrimp or prawns turn pink, about 10 minutes.

Remove from heat and puree in batches in a food processor or blender. Return to low heat and add the cream, sherry, tabasco, salt, pepper and lemon juice. Cook for another 15 to 20 minutes to let flavours blend.

Garnish with chopped fresh parsley.

*We love using lobster paste in soups and sauces. It's an intense, flavourful addition to many seafood recipes. It may seem expensive but you only need a little bit to make a big difference and·it will last in your freezer for a long time. You can find it at Railway Station Specialty Meats and Deli or most large food wholesaler companies such as Sysco Foods.

CHINESE BEEF AND CELERY NOODLE SOUP

Inspired by a fiery noodle soup from a restaurant in Vancouver's Chinatown, our version, though still hot, has been toned down to please the whole family. Using leftover or deli roast beef makes this soup easy and super quick.

- SERVES 6 -

INGREDIENTS

1 package 16 oz (454 g) thin, fresh chow mein noodles*
2 tbsp (30 ml) oil
1 medium onion, finely diced
3 cloves garlic, finely diced
2 tbsp (30 ml) grated fresh ginger
5 stalks celery, finely chopped
4 cups (1 L) low sodium beef broth
3 cups (750 ml) water
1/4 cup (60 ml) soy sauce
1/4 cup (60 ml) hoisin sauce
1/4 cup (60 ml) rice wine vinegar
1 tbsp (15 ml) sambal oelek (hot sauce)
1 tsp (5 ml) chinese 5 spice
1 pound or (500 g) cooked roast beef, julienned
2 tbsp (30 ml) sesame oil
4 green onions, julienned for garnish
1/2 small mild red chili, seeded and julienned for garnish

METHOD

Cook the noodles by plunging into boiling water for 2 minutes. Drain and set aside.
Heat the oil in a heavy bottomed soup pot. Add onions and brown over medium high heat.
Add garlic, ginger, and celery and continue cooking until vegetables are softened.
Add beef broth, water, soy sauce, hoisin sauce, rice wine vinegar, sambal oelek and chinese 5 spice. Bring to a simmer.
Add the roast beef and sesame oil and simmer for about 5 minutes more, no longer or the beef may get tough.
Taste for seasoning. The soup should be quite intense as the noodles will tone everything down.
Put some of the cooked noodles in a bowl and pour the hot soup over top.
Serve garnished with the julienned green onion and red chilies. If your guests like it hot, pass around a little more sambal oelek chili sauce.

*These are the fresh egg noodles that you can find in the produce section of your grocery store.

CHICKEN AND WILD RICE SOUP WITH PINEAPPLE CURRANT CHUTNEY

We devoured this bowl of beauty at a spectacular lodge near Winthrop, Washington on a mountain biking trip in the fall. It's rich and flavourful and really warms up the tired old legs at the end of a big ride. We think the chutney is essential and you will have more than you need, but it's delicious, and great for any kind of curry or to fancy up a plain old grilled chicken.

- SERVES 8 -

INGREDIENTS

1/2 cup (125 ml) butter
1/2 cup (125 ml) flour
4 cups (1 L) low sodium chicken stock
1 can (400 ml) coconut milk
3/4 cup (175 ml) pineapple juice
1 bay leaf
2 tbsp (30 ml) olive oil
1 medium onion, diced
1 cup (250 ml) celery, diced
2 large (500 g) boneless, skinless chicken breasts, cut into bite sized pieces
1 tsp (5 ml) garlic, crushed
1 tsp (5 ml) fresh ginger, finely chopped
1 tsp (5 ml) cumin
2 tbsp (30 ml) indian curry paste*
1 tsp (5 ml) curry powder
1 cup (250 ml) whipping cream
2 tbsp (30 ml) sweet chili sauce
1 tsp (5 ml) black pepper
1 tsp (5 ml) salt
1 cup (250 ml) cooked wild rice**
1/4 cup (60 ml) toasted almonds for garnish
Pineapple Currant Chutney for garnish (recipe on Page 82)

METHOD

Melt the butter in a medium sized pot and whisk in the flour to make the roux. Cook for 2-3 minutes to make sure the flour gets a bit roasted for a better flavour.

Slowly add the chicken stock, coconut milk, pineapple juice and bay leaf, stirring constantly to avoid lumps.

Heat the oil in a heavy bottomed stockpot and add the onion and celery. Cook until the vegetables are softened.

Add the chicken pieces and cook until done, about 5 minutes and then add the garlic, ginger, cumin, curry paste and curry powder. Stir until everything is covered with the spices and then add the cream.

Stir well and reheat until simmering.

Add the thickened chicken stock mixture, the sweet chili sauce, pepper and salt.

Add the cooked wild rice and ladle into soup bowls.

Garnish with toasted almonds and a spoonful of chutney.

Serve with a crispy pappadom if you wish.

**To cook the wild rice, put 1/2 cup (125 ml) wild rice and 2 cups (500 ml) cold water in a pot and bring to a boil. Reduce heat, cover tightly and cook for 30 minutes. Turn off the heat and let it stand for 35 minutes until it reaches desired texture. Drain.
*Can be found at Ellison's Market.

PARSNIP AND GRANNY SMITH APPLE SOUP

A simple but tasty puree, the tart apple and the apple cider vinegar really enhances that wonderful, slightly spicy flavour of the parsnips. Even those who think they don't like parsnips will love this.

- SERVES 6 -

INGREDIENTS

1/4 cup (60 ml) butter
2 large leeks, the white and some of the green, diced
2 granny smith apples, peeled and chopped
1 1/2 lbs (750 g) parsnips, peeled and chopped
2 shallots or 1/2 medium onion, minced
4 cups (1 L) low sodium chicken stock or vegetable stock*
1/2 cup (125 ml) whipping cream
1 tbsp (15 ml) apple cider vinegar
salt and pepper to taste

METHOD

Melt butter in a large heavy bottomed pot. Add leeks, apples, parsnips and shallots (or onions).
Sauté, stirring for about 10 minutes until everything is softened.
Add 4 cups (1 L) chicken or vegetable stock and simmer for about 30 minutes until everything is very tender. Let it cool for 5 minutes.
Puree in a food processor or blender until very smooth, you will need to do this in 2 batches. Put the pureed soup back in your soup pot.
Heat the soup on medium heat adding the cream and apple cider vinegar.
Taste and season for salt and pepper.

*Low sodium chicken and beef stock is widely available in handy (1 L) tetra pack containers. If you use regular stock be careful when doing your final seasoning, you may only need to add pepper. If you happen to have your own homemade stock - even better!

CHILLED ASPARAGUS SOUP WITH GOAT CHEESE CROSTINI

This creamy cold soup is such a refreshing way to begin a summer dinner. We like to make this in the spring when we can get gorgeous, fresh asparagus from the Creston Valley.

- SERVES 8 -

INGREDIENTS

2 lbs (1 kg) asparagus
1/4 cup (60 ml) butter
4 stalks celery, diced
1 fennel bulb, trimmed, cored and diced
2 leeks, finely chopped
2 potatoes, peeled and diced
6 cups (1.5 L) low sodium chicken stock or vegetable stock
1 cup (250 ml) white wine
1 cup (250 ml) whipping cream
1 tbsp (15 ml) fresh lemon juice
salt and pepper to taste
1 baguette
3.5 oz (100 g) goat cheese (1 small log)
1 garlic clove, cut in half
1/2 cup (125 ml) olive oil

METHOD

Trim tough ends of asparagus and discard, coarsely chop the remaining.

Melt the butter in a soup pot and sauté the celery, fennel, leeks, asparagus, and potatoes until soft.

Add stock and white wine and bring to a boil. Turn down the heat and simmer uncovered for half an hour, until vegetables are very tender. Remove from heat and let cool for 5 minutes.

Puree in a food processor or blender until smooth. Add whipping cream, lemon juice, salt and pepper to taste. Return to heat and cook for 5-10 minutes more.

Pour soup into a container and refrigerate until cool.

Preheat oven to 350°F (180°C).

Slice baguette into rounds and brush with olive oil on both sides.

Toast until crostini is light brown on top. Flip each crostini over to brown the other side. Remove from oven and rub each one with the halved garlic clove.

Place a spoonful of goat cheese on each crostini and broil until cheese is golden brown.

Ladle chilled soup into bowls and top each with a goat cheese crostini.

When asparagus is in season, we'd recommend buying lots. To freeze for use throughout the year just steam, cool and wrap tightly in a resealable plastic bag and store in your freezer.

NAT'S ROASTED MUSHROOM SOUP

A Fresh Tracks Café line cook extraordinaire, Nat Wansink's enthusiasm and charisma made him lots of friends and fans during his time in the kitchen. His version of a classic Mushroom Soup is a Whitewater favourite. And as Nat says, "don't hold back on the pepper!"

- SERVES 8 -

INGREDIENTS

2 tbsp (30 ml) vegetable oil
1 medium sized onion, diced
5 cloves garlic, chopped
1 tbsp (15 ml) fresh rosemary, chopped
1 1/2 lbs (750 g) mushrooms, thickly sliced
1/3 cup (75 ml) butter
1/3 cup (75 ml) flour
1/2 tsp (2 ml) ground thyme
4 cups (1 L) milk
2 cups (500 ml) low sodium chicken stock or vegetable stock
1 tsp (5 ml) fresh rosemary, chopped
salt and pepper to taste

METHOD

Preheat oven to 375°F (190°C).
Heat the oil in a large heavy bottomed pot over medium heat. Add the onions and cook for a few minutes until softened. Add garlic and fresh rosemary and sauté for a few minutes more.
Add all the mushrooms and toss everything well to combine.
Spread the mushroom and onion mixture out on a baking sheet and put in the hot 375°F (190°C) oven for about 25 minutes, stirring once or twice. The mushrooms should be tender and starting to turn golden brown. Remove from oven and cool slightly.
Melt the butter in the heavy bottomed pot (no need to wash it) and add the flour, stirring to make a roux. Add the ground thyme and cook the roux for a couple of minutes.
Pour in the milk slowly, whisking to prevent lumps. Simmer over medium low heat for about 5 minutes until thickened.
Add half of the mushroom and onion mixture and chicken stock to your food processor or blender. Purée until very smooth. Add the purée and the rest of the mushroom and onion mixture to the soup pot. Stir to combine and bring the soup up to a simmer for a few minutes.
Season with 1 tsp (5 ml) fresh rosemary, salt and lots of freshly ground black pepper.

Use any variety or combination of mushrooms that you like. A few chanterelles or portobellos would be great.

BAKED SPAGHETTI SQUASH

This is just the thing to serve with a big turkey and mashed potato dinner. It's simple and light, a pleasant relief from all the richness. Last Thanksgiving dinner, a meal that usually produces lots of good leftovers, the only dish that was completely consumed was this humble yet scrumptious baked squash.

- SERVES 6 -

INGREDIENTS

1 spaghetti squash (about 2 lbs or 1 kg)
1/4 cup (60 ml) butter
1/2 cup (125 ml) parmesan, freshly grated
juice of 1 lemon
1/4 cup (60 ml) flat leafed parsley, chopped
1/2 tsp (2 ml) nutmeg, freshly grated
1 tsp (5 ml) salt
1 tsp (5 ml) pepper

METHOD

Cut the squash in half and scoop out the seeds with a metal spoon.
Place the squash skin side up on a baking tray, pour about a cup of water over and cover with tin foil or a lid.
Bake at 350°F (180°C) for 45 minutes or until the squash feels soft when you squeeze it.
Remove from the oven and let cool for a few minutes. Scrape out long strands of the squash into a baking dish using a fork.
Mix in the butter, parmesan, lemon juice, parsley, nutmeg, salt and pepper.
Cover and keep warm until ready to serve.

You could make this the day before you wish to serve it and reheat it just before serving. This comes in handy if you have a crowd coming over and you want to spend the day on the slopes or your bike!

BARLEY MUSHROOM RISOTTO

It's always good to have a few yummy side dishes that aren't potatoes, rice or pasta.
This homey, hearty risotto will pair perfectly with your favourite comfort food.

- SERVES 4 AS A SIDE DISH -

INGREDIENTS

2 cups (500 ml) low sodium vegetable or chicken stock
1 cup (250 ml) white wine
1/4 cup (60 ml) olive oil
1 cup (250 ml) pearl barley
1/2 medium onion, diced
2 garlic cloves, crushed
1 cup (250 ml) mushrooms, sliced
1/4 cup (60 ml) parmesan cheese, grated
salt and freshly ground black pepper to taste
1/4 cup (60 ml) fresh parsley, chopped

METHOD

Combine vegetable stock and wine and heat until simmering.
Heat olive oil in a heavy bottomed pot and sauté barley until slightly toasted, about 5 minutes.
Add onion and garlic and cook until transparent. Add the mushrooms and sauté for another 5 minutes.
Add the hot stock half a cup at a time, stirring until all the liquid has been absorbed into the barley, about 30 minutes.
Test a kernel of barley for doneness. It should be al dente; if it's still too firm you may need to add another 1/2 cup (125 ml) of water, and continue cooking until done.
Turn heat off and stir in the parmesan cheese.
Place a lid on the pot and let sit for about 5 minutes.
Season with salt, freshly ground black pepper and chopped parsley.

This is particularly good with our Braised Lamb Shanks on Page 101.

MARNI'S ROASTED CORN AND FETA

This is perfect for one of those days that you want to cook the whole dinner on the barbeque and stay out of the kitchen as much as possible. This comes from Marni, an annual summertime visitor to Nelson and a great and inventive home cook.

- SERVES 6 -

INGREDIENTS

6 ears of fresh corn in husks
2 red peppers
1/2 cup (125 ml) butter (or olive oil)
4 cloves garlic, minced
1 tsp (5 ml) ground cumin
1/2 cup (125 ml) cilantro, chopped
1/2 cup (125 ml) feta cheese, crumbled
juice of 2 fresh limes
salt and pepper to taste
1 lime for garnish
cilantro sprigs for garnish

METHOD

Soak corn in cold water to cover for at least an hour, longer if you can.
Heat barbeque to low and place corn in husks on grill and cook for about 45 minutes.
Place the whole red peppers on the barbeque as well. Turn them as needed and let them get really charred. They'll take about 20 minutes.
Remove red peppers from grill, peel the charred skins off and take out the core and stems and dice.
Melt butter and add minced garlic.
Remove husks from cooked corn and slice off all the kernels. Place in mixing bowl and add the cumin, cilantro, feta, lime juice, diced roasted peppers and melted garlic butter. Season with salt and pepper to taste. Toss to combine.
Transfer to a serving bowl and garnish with fresh limes and cilantro sprigs.

Try making this with olive oil instead of the melted butter and serve it as a salad.

PINEAPPLE AND CURRANT CHUTNEY

We think it's mandatory that a spoonful of this chutney be served on top of our Curried Chicken and Wild Rice Soup. Give this a try as a tasty addition to your next baked ham.

- MAKES ABOUT 2 CUPS (500 ML) -

INGREDIENTS

1 lemon, juice and zest of
2 tsp (10 ml) fresh ginger, finely chopped
1/2 cup (125 ml) sugar
1/2 cup (125 ml) water
2 tbsp (30 ml) olive oil
1 medium onion, diced
2 cups (500 ml) fresh pineapple, diced
1 cup (250 ml) pineapple juice
2 tbsp (30 ml) sugar
1 tsp (5 ml) nutmeg
1 tsp (5 ml) cinnamon
1/2 tsp (2 ml) ground cloves
1/4 cup (60 ml) rice wine vinegar
3/4 cup (175 ml) dried currants

METHOD

Place lemon juice and zest, ginger, sugar and water in a small saucepan on medium high heat.
Reduce by half until mixture is a thick syrup. Set aside.
Heat olive oil in heavy bottomed pan and sauté onion until translucent.
Add pineapple, pineapple juice, sugar, nutmeg, cinnamon, cloves, vinegar and currants.
Cook mixture on low heat until reduced and thick, about ½ hour.
Add lemon/ginger syrup and stir to combine.

Store in an airtight container in the fridge for up to a week.
Curried Chicken and Wild Rice Soup can be found on page 72.

GWEN'S PLUM SAUCE

This fruity, bold condiment is perfect with any kind of roasted meat or as a dip for chicken strips. The delightful Gwen Cavanaugh passed this on to us and now we make it every year.

- MAKES ABOUT 6 PINT (500 ML) JARS -

INGREDIENTS

2 lbs (1 kg) apples, peeled and chopped
2 lbs (1 kg) plums, pitted and chopped
1 1/2 cups (375 ml) water
1 large onion, roughly chopped
1 1/2 cups (375 ml) malt vinegar
2 tsp (10 ml) ground ginger
1 tsp (5 ml) ground nutmeg
1 tsp (5 ml) allspice
1/2 tsp (2 ml) cayenne pepper
3 tbsp (45 ml) pickling salt
2 3/4 cups (650 ml) brown sugar

METHOD

Put the apples, plums, onion and water into a large (6 L) heavy bottomed pot. Cook and stir for about 30 minutes on medium heat until everything is softened.

Cool slightly and transfer to a food processor and puree until quite smooth. You will need to do this in 2 or 3 batches. You can also do this with a hand blender right in the pot.

Add all remaining ingredients and bring the mixture to a boil.

Simmer on very low, stirring, for a couple of hours until it becomes a thick sauce.

Put sealing lids in a pot of water and boil for 5 minutes.

Ladle the plum sauce into sterilized jam jars and seal.

This condiment is a great little addition when making sauces or gravies for lamb or pork.

WASHING MACHINE DILL PICKLES

Sounds a little nuts but we've been making pickles like this for years. It's just so easy and they are truly the crunchiest dills you've ever tasted.

- EACH POUND OF PICKLES MAKES ABOUT 1 QUART JAR -

INGREDIENTS

8 lbs (about 3 1/2 kg) pickling cucumbers
4 cups (1 L) Heinz white pickling vinegar
12 cups (3 L) water
3/4 cup (175 ml) pickling salt
2 bunches fresh dill or 8 heads dill weed (or a little of both)

METHOD

Put the cucumbers in the washing machine and run them through a gentle wash cycle. After they drain, fill the machine with cold water and soak the cucumbers overnight.

In the morning spin the cucumbers dry and remove from the washing machine. You can also wash the cucumbers in a sink, drain it, fill it with cold water and leave overnight.

Preheat the oven to 200°F (100°C).

Sterilize 8 (1 quart) canning jars by washing them in the dishwasher then putting them on a tea towel lined baking pan in the oven for 20 minutes. Keep them in the oven.

Put 8 lids and the rims in a pot of water to cover and bring to a boil for 10 minutes to sterilize.

Make the brine by combining the vinegar, water and pickling salt in a large pot over medium high heat. Bring the brine to a rapid boil.

Take one jar out of the oven at a time, packing some dill into the bottom of the jar then filling with cucumbers.

Cover with the simmering brine.

Seal with sterilized hot lids making sure to clean the rim of any residue with a clean cloth.

The success of these pickles comes from the simplicity of the ingredients and working hot and fast. This recipe can easily be doubled and it's a great project for two pals. Just make sure you don't have a bunch of little kids running around the kitchen while you're juggling the hot jars and boiling brine. If any of your jars don't seal, store them in the fridge where they will keep for months.

ROASTED RED POTATOES WITH PANCETTA AND RED PEPPERS

This is one of those simple combinations that produces something special. The sweetness of the peppers and the salty smokiness of the pancetta turns these roast potatoes into a real treat.

- SERVES 6 -

INGREDIENTS

¹/4 cup (60 ml) olive oil

2 lbs (1 kg) red nugget potatoes, halved or quartered

150 g pancetta, cubed

2 red peppers, chopped into 1 inch (2.5 cm) pieces

4 cloves garlic, minced

2 tsp (10 ml) coarse salt

2 tsp (10 ml) pepper, freshly ground

METHOD

Heat oil on a heavy baking sheet in a preheated 400°F (200°C) oven for a few minutes until hot but not smoking.

Toss together the potatoes, pancetta, red peppers, garlic, salt and pepper.

Remove the pan from the oven and spread the potatoes, pancetta and peppers carefully into the hot oil.

Bake at 400°F (200°C) for about 30 minutes until the potatoes are golden and the pancetta is crisp.

Serve these potatoes with Roast Leg of Lamb with Cinzano Rosemary demi-glace on Page 126.

WOK SEARED GREEN BEANS AND JAPANESE EGGPLANT

When you are looking for a vegetable dish that is different and intensely flavoured, this is a good one. It's also one of those things that is good to have in your fridge for a snack the next day.

- SERVES 8 -

INGREDIENTS

1/2 cup (125 ml) vegetable oil

4 japanese eggplants, unpeeled and cut into 3 inch (7.50 cm) long, 1/2 inch (1.25 cm) wide strips

1 lb (500 g) green beans, trimmed

2 red peppers, halved and sliced lengthwise

2 tbsp (30 ml) garlic, minced

1 tbsp (15 ml) fresh ginger, grated and chopped

2 tbsp (30 ml) yellow miso paste mixed with 2/3 cup (150 ml) water

2 tbsp (30 ml) soy sauce

2 tsp (10 ml) thai red curry paste

1/2 cup (125 ml) fresh mint or cilantro, chopped for garnish

METHOD

Heat oil in wok or heavy skillet over medium high heat until hot but not smoking.

Add eggplant strips and toss to coat with oil. Stir fry until eggplant strips begin to brown, about 2 minutes.

Add green beans and red peppers and stir fry until they are crisp and tender, about 4 minutes.

Add garlic and ginger and stir fry, about 10 seconds.

Add miso mixture, soy sauce and curry paste and stir until liquids thicken and coat vegetables, about 2 minutes.

Turn off the heat, sprinkle with chopped cilantro or mint, and serve.

Julienned tofu is also a great addition and turns this into a complete vegetarian meal.

GRILLED VEGETABLE STACKS

Layers of beautifully grilled vegetables held together with fresh mozzarella and pesto. Make these in the summer when our local produce is at it's best.

- SERVES 8 -

INGREDIENTS

1 cup (250 ml) pesto sauce, homemade or store bought

2 japanese eggplants

2 red peppers, quartered and seeded

2 yellow peppers, quartered and seeded

2 yams, peeled

2 zucchinis

2 red onions

2 tomatoes

1/2 cup (125 ml) olive oil

1/4 cup (60 ml) balsamic vinegar

1 cup (250 ml) grated mozzarella or sliced fresh mozzarella (bocconcini)

1/2 cup (125 ml) goat cheese

8-six inch wooden skewers

8 sprigs fresh rosemary

1/4 cup (60 ml) balsamic crema*

METHOD

Slice eggplants, yams, zucchini, red onions and tomatoes into 1/4 inch slices (0.5 cm)

Brush all vegetables, except tomatoes, with olive oil and balsamic vinegar.

Heat barbeque to medium and grill all vegetables except tomatoes until they have some nice grill marks and are tender. You could also roast the vegetables in a 350°F (180°C) oven until all the vegetables are tender, about 20 minutes.

Assemble 8 vegetable stacks by layering slices of vegetables with pesto and cheeses between the layers. Start the stacks with the yams and finish with the zucchini. Place a wooden skewer in the middle of each stack.

Make ahead and reheat in a 350°F (180°C) oven or the barbeque for approximately 20 minutes to melt the cheese and heat the vegetables. Once heated, remove the skewers and replace with sprigs of fresh rosemary.

Serve the stacks drizzled with some of the balsamic crema.

If you're looking for a really beautiful show-stopping vegetable dish to place next to a perfectly grilled steak or fish filet, this is the one. It also works well as a vegetarian entrée...
*balsamic crema is a wonderful, sweet, tart and syrupy reduction of balsamic vinegar and concentrated grape juice. It adds a luxuriously delicious flavour to all kinds of food. It's packaged in a handy squeeze bottle for drizzling and can be found locally at The Railway Station Specialty Meats and Deli.

DINNERS

HALIBUT WITH A WASABI PEA CRUST

Halibut is one of our favourite fish to prepare, and to eat. It's very versatile because of the subtle but rich flavour and texture. This crust with a Japanese flair has just the right amount of zip and crunch to contrast with the moist fish.

- SERVES 6 -

INGREDIENTS

2 1/2 lbs (1.25 kg) fresh halibut fillet
1 cup (250 ml) mayonnaise
3 tbsp (45 ml) sweet chili sauce
1 1/2 cups (375 ml) wasabi peas* chopped roughly by hand or in a food processor

METHOD

Preheat oven to 400°F (200°C).
Cut halibut into 6 equal pieces.
Mix the mayonnaise and the sweet chili sauce together in a small bowl.
Put the halibut pieces, evenly spaced, onto a baking sheet lined with parchment paper.
Spread mayonnaise mixture evenly on the top of each piece of halibut.
Press the chopped wasabi peas firmly into the mayonnaise and sweet chili coating on the halibut.
Bake in 400°F (200°C) oven for about 15 to 20 minutes, until halibut starts to flake and peas start to brown slightly.
Serve right away.

Halibut will continue to cook a bit after it has been taken out of the oven, so be sure to take it out just when it's starting to look opaque and flaky.

The key to delicious fish is timing. Make sure your table is set, and the rest of the meal ready to go. The fish should come right out of the oven and on to the plates. The rule of thumb for cooking time is 8 minutes of cooking time per inch of thickness. So if the fillet is 2 inches thick the cooking time will be about 16 minutes.

With a bit of practise and using the thickness formula, you will attain fish perfection every time! Happy perfect fish eating!

*Wasabi peas are dried peas, roasted and coated with wasabi. They are available packaged or in bulk at your grocery store.

CHICKEN TORTILLA PIE

This is really just chicken enchiladas made easy, with a much prettier presentation. You should try to assemble it the day before, not only will it taste even better but it will also cut and serve better too.

- SERVES 8 TO 12 -

INGREDIENTS

1-10 inch (25 cm) spring form pan
6-10 inch (25 cm) flour tortillas
2 tbsp (30 ml) canola oil
2 onions, thinly sliced
2 red peppers, thinly sliced
6 chicken breasts, boneless, skinless and thinly sliced or 2 lbs (1 kg) ground chicken meat
1 tbsp (15 ml) seasoning salt
2 tsp (10 ml) cumin
1 tsp (5 ml) oregano
1 tsp (5 ml) chili powder
1/2 cup (125 ml) cream cheese
1/2 cup (125 ml) sour cream
2 cups (500 ml) monterey jack cheese, grated
1/2 cup (125 ml) fresh cilantro, chopped
1/4 cup (60 ml) chopped canned jalapeno peppers
1 cup (250 ml) cheddar cheese, grated
2 -(398 ml) cans refried beans
1 can (283 g) enchilada sauce (La Victoria is best)

A layer of grilled zucchini or red peppers would give this pie some beautiful colour and texture if you felt like getting some vegetables in there. This is really hard to describe! Basically you have 6 tortillas, 3 layers of chicken and two layers of beans....Salud!

METHOD

Heat the oil in a large frying pan over medium heat.
Saute the onions and peppers for about 10 minutes until softened.
Add the sliced chicken and cook until chicken is just cooked, about 15 minutes.
Add seasoning salt, cumin, oregano, chili powder and saute for another 3 to 4 minutes. Remove from heat and add the cream cheese, sour cream and 1 cup (250 ml) monterey jack cheese.
Stir until combined.
Mix in the cilantro and jalapeno peppers.
Brush a flour tortilla on both sides with some of the enchilada sauce. Lay tortilla in the bottom of an oiled spring form pan.
Spread a layer of chicken mixture on top. You will need to make 3 layers so only use 1/3 of the mix. Brush another tortilla with enchilada sauce and place on top. Press down with your fingers to glue the layers together a bit.
Spread this layer with one can of the refried beans, the other can is for another layer. Sprinkle with a 1/3 cup (75 ml) of the remaining cheese and top with another tortilla that has been brushed with enchilada sauce.
Continue to alternate layers of the chicken mixture with beans and cheese using the remaining 3 tortillas and enchilada sauce. Top the pie with remaining monterey jack and cheddar and cover with tin foil.
Bake in 350°F (180°C) oven for 1 hour. Remove foil and bake for another 15 to 20 minutes. Take the pie out of the oven and let it rest for about 15 minutes.
Slice the pie into wedges and serve on top of a bed of shredded lettuce. Top with sour cream, fresh cilantro, diced avocado and salsa.

GRILLED STEAK WITH OVEN ROASTED TOMATOES, BLUE CHEESE AND RED WINE DEMI-GLACE

Decadent but simple and perfect for any season, this one will knock the socks off you and your guests! In the summer serve it on top of some beautiful fresh spinach or baby greens. In the winter, on a bed of garlic mashed potatoes.

- SERVES 6 -

OVEN ROASTED TOMATOES

6 tomatoes, cut into 1/2 inch (1.25 cm) thick slices
1 tsp (5 ml) salt
1 tsp (5 ml) pepper
1 tsp (5 ml) sugar

RED WINE DEMI-GLACE

2 tbsp (30 ml) butter
4 shallots, diced
2 garlic cloves, minced
1/4 cup (60 ml) celery, diced small
1/4 cup (60 ml) red wine vinegar
1/2 cup (125 ml) red wine
1/4 cup (60 ml) fresh thyme, roughly chopped
1/4 cup (60 ml) fresh rosemary, roughly chopped
2 cups (500 ml) demi-glace

INGREDIENTS

6 sirloin or filet mignon steaks
2 tbsp (30 ml) olive oil
salt and pepper
1/2 cup (125 ml) blue cheese, crumbled
sprigs of fresh rosemary for garnish

METHOD

Place tomato slices on two parchment paper lined baking pans, sprinkle with salt, pepper and sugar.
Roast in 325°F (160°C) oven for about 1 hour until tomatoes are slightly caramelized.
Remove from the oven and set aside.

Melt 2 tbsp (30 ml) butter in heavy bottomed saucepan over low heat.
Add shallots, garlic and celery and sauté until soft.
Pour in vinegar and reduce until absorbed into shallot mixture, about 10 minutes.
Add the wine, thyme and rosemary and reduce by half.
Add the demi-glace and simmer for about 1/2 an hour.
Strain and keep warm on medium heat. If you prefer a thicker sauce, mix together 2 tbsp (30 ml) cold butter and 2 tbsp (30 ml) flour and whisk until incorporated.

Preheat barbeque or grill pan to medium high heat.
Brush steaks with olive oil, salt and pepper and cook until desired doneness. Rest the steaks for about 10 minutes.
Serve by placing steak on individual plates topped with slices of roasted tomato, crumbled blue cheese and warm sauce.
Garnish with sprigs of fresh rosemary.

The Railway Station Specialty Meats and Deli not only carries beautiful meat and fish but they also carry demi-glace. Good demi-glace is a handy thing to have for all your sauce making.
A grill pan is our favourite new piece of low tech cooking equipment. It is basically a type of frying pan with raised ridges usually made from enamel coated cast iron. It's really great for cooking a couple of steaks or a small fillet of fish and ideal for grilling vegetables and fruit. Available at Cottonwood Kitchens.

CHICKEN ASIAGO

While this cozy classic is usually reserved for family dinners, who wouldn't love to sit down with good friends and tuck into this? This is when your homemade tomato sauce makes all the difference.

- SERVES 6 -

INGREDIENTS

6 chicken breasts, boneless, skinless and pounded slightly
1 tsp (5 ml) salt
1 tsp (5 ml) pepper
1/3 cup (75 ml) flour
2 eggs, slightly beaten with 1 tbsp (15 ml) water
1 1/2 cups (375 ml) panko or other dry bread crumbs
1/2 cup (125 ml) asiago, freshly grated, divided
1 tsp (5 ml) dried oregano
2 tbsp (30 ml) flat leaf parsley, finely chopped
1/4 cup (60 ml) olive oil or vegetable oil
2 cups (500 ml) tomato sauce (good quality store bought or homemade)
7 oz (200 g) fresh mozzarella, sliced
1/2 cup (125 ml) fresh basil leaves, chopped

METHOD

Season the pounded chicken breasts with salt and pepper.
Prepare 3 bowls, one with flour, one with egg and water mixture and one with bread crumbs, 1/4 cup (60 ml) asiago, oregano and parsley.
Dredge each breast in flour, then dip in the egg, shake off excess and dip in the bread crumbs. Press the crumbs in.
Heat the olive oil or vegetable oil to medium high heat in a large sauté pan. Saute the chicken breasts until they are golden brown.
Place in a shallow baking pan and cover each piece of chicken with tomato sauce. Top with slices of mozzarella and chopped basil. Sprinkle with remaining asiago.
Bake in a 350°F (180°C) oven for about 30 minutes until cheese is golden and chicken is cooked through.
Serve with any kind of pasta and a crisp green salad.

Big Red Tomato Sauce can be found on Page 110.

BRAISED LAMB SHANKS

If you are planning on spending the afternoon at home on a chilly fall or winter day, this is the perfect thing to have simmering away in the oven. Shelley's brother Chris makes this for dinner often because he can tick a few chores off his list, like raking the leaves or shoveling the snow, and have a delicious dinner ready for his daughters at the end of the day.

- SERVES 4 -

INGREDIENTS

4 lamb shanks
1/2 cup (125 ml) flour
1 tsp (5 ml) salt
1 tsp (5 ml) pepper
1/4 cup (60 ml) olive oil
2 onions, diced
4 cloves garlic, minced
1 1/2 cups (375 ml) celery, diced
1 1/2 cups (375 ml) red wine
1-28 oz (796 ml) can tomatoes
2 carrots, diced
2 cups (500 ml) low sodium beef stock
2 tbsp (30 ml) tomato paste
1 bay leaf
2 tsp (10 ml) fresh thyme
2 tbsp (30 ml) parsley, chopped for garnish

METHOD

Mix the flour with the salt and pepper in a medium sized bowl.

Dredge the lamb shanks in flour mixture to coat.

Heat oil in a large heavy bottomed, ovenproof pot over medium high heat. Add the lamb shanks and brown on all sides.

Remove lamb from pot and set aside. Turn heat down to medium; add more oil if needed and add chopped onion, garlic and celery. Sauté until softened.

Add the wine to deglaze the pan (this will loosen up all the bits stuck to the bottom and incorporate them into your stew).

Add tomatoes, carrots, beef stock, tomato paste, bay leaf and thyme. Stir well. Add the browned shanks back into the pot, covering them with the liquid.

Braise, covered, in a 325°F (160°C) oven for at least 2 1/2 to 3 hours, turning the shanks around a couple of times during cooking. When the shanks are done the meat should be almost falling off the bone.

Serve garnished with chopped parsley.

This would be delicious with our Barley Risotto on Page 80 or some plain, buttered egg noodles.

CHICKEN SALTIMBOCCA

Looking for an easy dinner that you can fling together in half an hour that everyone loves?
We always are! Paired with a simple, fresh pasta dish, it can turn a monday night chicken
breast into a casual Tuscan style feast.

- SERVES 6 -

INGREDIENTS

six medium sized chicken breasts, boneless, skinless
1 tsp (5 ml) salt
1 tsp (5 ml) pepper
12 fresh sage leaves
6 prosciutto slices, big enough to wrap each chicken breast
1/4 cup (60 ml) olive oil
1/2 cup (125 ml) marsala, wine or port
juice of 1 lemon

METHOD

Place chicken breasts on work surface and season with salt and pepper.
Put 2 sage leaves on top of each breast.
Wrap a slice of prosciutto around each breast, covering the sage leaves and overlapping the ends of the prosciutto. Skewer with a toothpick.
Heat oil in large ovenproof sauté pan over medium heat. Place chicken in pan and just cook until seared and brown on each side.
Finish cooking in 350°F (180°C) oven, for about 15 to 20 minutes, or until juices run clear out of chicken.
Remove the chicken from the oven and return the pan to stovetop over medium heat.
Add the wine and let it "deglaze" the pan. Stir in the lemon juice and remove from heat.
Slice the chicken on the diagonal for a pretty presentation.
Pour the pan sauce over the top of the chicken.

We recommend serving this with the Summertime Pasta on Page 122.

CRISPY TOFU NUGGETS

A good way to get everyone eating more tofu. Kids and grown ups will gobble these up as fast as you can get them out of the pan. Bring out the ketchup or any favourite dipping sauce.

- SERVES 4 -

INGREDIENTS

1 package 15.50 oz (440 g) regular tofu
2 tbsp (30 ml) soy sauce
1 tsp (5 ml) sesame oil
1 tbsp (15 ml) rice vinegar
1 tbsp (15 ml) thai sweet chili sauce
1 tbsp (15 ml) cornstarch
1 tbsp (15 ml) water
1/3 cup (75 ml) raw sesame seeds
or 1/3 cup (75 ml) panko or other dry breadcrumbs
2 tbsp (30 ml) vegetable oil for frying

METHOD

Slice a block of tofu into 5 square slices then cut each square into 3 rectangles. You should have 15 pieces.
Put the tofu in the bottom of a glass baking dish.
Mix together the soy sauce, sesame oil, rice vinegar and sweet chili sauce; pour this over the tofu turning pieces around to coat.
Marinate for about an hour (or longer) turning the tofu over a couple of times.
Mix the cornstarch and water together in a small bowl.
Put the sesame seeds or panko bread crumbs in another small bowl.
Remove the tofu from the marinade, (most likely, it will be all absorbed in to the tofu) and dip each piece first into the cornstarch mixture and then the seeds or crumbs, pressing quite firmly to get them to stick.
Heat a sauté pan to medium and add the vegetable oil.
Add the tofu nuggets to the hot pan and sauté for a minute or 2 on each side until they are golden brown. Don't try to fit too many in the pan at one time or you'll have trouble flipping them around.
Remove from the pan and serve right away with your favourite dipping sauces.

In the Kootenays we like to use Silverking Tofu. It's made locally and available all over town.

LAMB CHOPS WITH PORT PLUM SAUCE AND TOMATO ARUGULA SALAD

When the Dance Umbrella divas get together to plan their spring showcase and share a well deserved meal, this is what they like to eat. Savoury lamb, a light salad and lots and lots of rich, fruity, port spiked sauce.

- SERVES 4 -

PORT PLUM SAUCE

1 tbsp (15 ml) vegetable oil
2 shallots or 1/2 medium white onion, diced
1 cup (250 ml) port wine
1 cup (250 ml) low sodium chicken stock
1/4 cup (60 ml) plum sauce
2 tbsp (30 ml) butter

INGREDIENTS

2 racks of lamb (about 450 g)
2 eggs
1 tbsp (15 ml) dijon mustard
1 tsp (5 ml) salt
1 tsp (5 ml) pepper, freshly ground
1 cup (250 ml) panko or other dry breadcrumbs
1/4 cup (60 ml) freshly grated parmesan
1/4 cup (60 ml) vegetable oil for frying

SALAD

4 roma tomatoes
6 cups (1.5 L) arugula
juice of 1 lemon
1/4 cup (60 ml) olive oil
1/2 tsp (2 ml) salt
1/2 tsp (2 ml) pepper

METHOD

Heat the oil and sauté the shallots or onion in a small saucepan until softened.
Add the port and chicken stock, simmer to reduce by half.
Add the plum sauce and butter, whisking to incorporate.
Keep the sauce warm until you need it or make it ahead without the butter. Refrigerate it and add the butter when you warm it up.
Cut the lamb into riblets or have your butcher do it for you.
Trim any thick fat off the lamb and pound the pieces until the meaty part is about half as thick.
Beat together the egg, mustard, salt and pepper in a small bowl.
Mix the breadcrumbs and parmesan together in another small bowl.
Dip the chops into the egg mixture then press them into the crumbs. Put them on a plate and sprinkle with any remaining crumbs. Refrigerate until needed.
Heat 1/4 cup (60 ml) vegetable oil in a large frying pan until hot but not smoking.
Place chops carefully in the frying pan and cook for about 4 minutes on each side. They should be evenly golden brown.
Cut the tomatoes into half moon shaped slices and toss with the arugula, lemon juice, olive oil and salt and pepper.
Place some of the salad on each plate and top it with the lamb chops.
Serve with the Port Plum Sauce on the side.

A single rack of lamb lends itself perfectly to an intimate dinner for two. Gwen's plum sauce found on Page 84.

EMMY'S MARRAKESH BOWL

Our wildly entertaining friend Emmy is a great cook and recreational food critic. She's always on the run so she likes to eat everything out of a soup bowl and often has a great recipe to share. This scrumptious stew is one of her favourites.

- SERVES 8 TO 10 -

INGREDIENTS

1/4 cup (60 ml) vegetable oil
3 lbs (1.5 kg) cubed beef, or lamb
1/2 cup (125 ml) flour
2 large onions, diced
2 garlic cloves, minced
1-28 oz (796 ml) can diced tomatoes
1 cup (250 ml) dry sherry
1/2 cup (125 ml) raisins
1 tsp (5 ml) turmeric
1 tsp (5 ml) hot chili flakes
1 tsp (5 ml) salt
1/2 tsp (2 ml) tarragon
1/2 tsp (2 ml) cinnamon
1/2 tsp (2ml) thyme
1/2 tsp (2 ml) allspice
1/2 tsp (2 ml) coriander
1/2 tsp (2 ml) ground cloves
1/2 tsp (2 ml) nutmeg
1 lb (500 g) carrots, diced
2 large red peppers, diced
2 large tomatoes, diced

METHOD

Heat the oil in a large pot.
Dredge the meat in flour and sauté in two batches until browned on all sides, set aside.
Add onions and garlic to the pot and sauté until translucent. Return meat to the pot.
Add tomatoes, sherry, raisins and all spices and let simmer for 45 minutes to an hour, stirring occasionally.
Add diced carrots, red peppers and fresh tomatoes.
Cook for 10 more minutes, or until carrots are just tender.
Serve in soup bowls.

This is great over couscous, rice or quinoa.

If you own a beautiful, big, heavy duty cast iron pot, use it. If you don't, go buy one! It'll inspire you to cook so many things. They come in many stunning colours and are available at Cottonwood Kitchens.

- 107 -

CEDAR PLANKED SALMON WITH MAPLE SOY GLAZE

This will give you a beautiful, moist, slightly smoky flavoured salmon and a wonderfully cedar scented backyard.

- SERVES 4 TO 6 -

INGREDIENTS

1-12 x 8 x 1 inch untreated cedar plank*
1/2 cup (125 ml) pure maple syrup
1/2 cup (125 ml) japanese soy sauce or tamari
2 lbs (about 1 kg) wild salmon fillet with skin on and pin bones out

METHOD

Soak the untreated cedar plank submerged in water for at least 4 hours or overnight.
Simmer the syrup and the soy on low heat for about 15 minutes until it reaches the consistency of honey.
Pour into a clean jar and cool completely.
Brush the salmon fillet with about 1/4 cup (60 ml) of the cooled glaze and marinate for an hour.
Preheat the barbeque on high.
Remove the plank from the water and place it on the grill to dry slightly for a minute.
Turn the barbeque down to low.
Put the fish skin side down on the plank tucking the tail in underneath it if it won't fit.
Close the barbeque lid and cook for about 15 to 20 minutes depending on the thickness of your salmon.
Brush on some more of the glaze a couple of times during cooking.
Serve the salmon right off the plank or slide it on to a platter (the skin usually stays on the plank).
Garnish with some grilled green onions.

Because the salmon is cooked more slowly and with moist heat from the cedar, it should not dry out like it can when barbequed right on the grill. This makes it much better to serve at room temperature.

*To have a supply of planks for your summertime barbequing, you can buy a whole plank of untreated cedar at your local lumberyard and have them cut it into your desired lengths. You can also buy singles at most kitchenware or grocery stores. This salmon would be great with any kind of salsa or chutney.

BIG RED TOMATO SAUCE

We all know that a lot of good things start with a really great tomato sauce. This is uncomplicated but so full of flavour, it will become a star in your repertoire. It's all about the tomatoes, so use the best.

- SERVES 6 -

INGREDIENTS

1/2 cup (125 ml) olive oil

4 cloves garlic, crushed

1 tsp (5 ml) dried red pepper flakes

3-28 oz (796 ml) cans of good tomatoes (italian plum)

1/2 cup (125 ml) red wine (optional)

2 tbsp (30 ml) red wine vinegar (if not using red wine)

2 tbsp (30 ml) dried oregano

1 tbsp (15 ml) brown sugar

1 tsp (5 ml) salt

1/2 cup (125 ml) fresh basil (if you have it)

METHOD

Heat the oil in a heavy bottomed pot and add the garlic and red pepper flakes for a minute being careful not to burn the garlic.

Put the tomatoes in a blender and pulse to break them up just a bit. You can also use your hands or a knife.

Add the tomatoes carefully (they may spatter and splash in the hot oil) and all the remaining ingredients.

Bring to a boil then reduce the heat to a nice low simmer and cook for an hour or so, stirring often.

If you want to use it for pizza sauce, reduce to a thicker consistency.

We make this a lot and recently used some canned tomatoes that had tons of added sodium, so check the label and taste before seasoning with salt.

FAMILY STYLE SUSHI

Last year Conner Adams went to Japan on a student exchange trip and came home with a new appreciation for the cuisine. This is how his host family often prepared sushi. Everyone can create their own roll and the work is shared equally. It can all be on the table in about half an hour and Mom doesn't have to do all the work, and we all like that.

- SERVES 4 -

INGREDIENTS

1/2 lb (250 g) wild salmon fillet
1/2 lb (250 g) ahi tuna
2 cups (500 ml) uncooked sushi rice
2 tbsp (30 ml) rice wine vinegar
1 tbsp (15 ml) sugar
1 tbsp (15 ml) wasabi paste
1/2 cup (125 ml) mayonnaise, divided
1 tbsp (15 ml) sweet chili sauce
1/2 cup (125 ml) sushi ginger
1 red pepper, julienned
1/2 cucumber, julienned
1 avocado, thinly sliced
1 cup (250 ml) sunflower sprouts
8 green onions, sliced lengthwise in half
1 package nori, 8 to 12 sheets
1/2 cup (125 ml) soy sauce for dipping
1/4 cup (60 ml) sesame seeds for garnish

METHOD

Preheat barbeque or grill pan to medium heat.
Prepare sushi rice according to package directions using 2 cups (500 ml) of rice.
Heat the sugar and vinegar and add to the cooked rice.
Mix together the wasabi and 1/4 cup (60 ml) of the mayonnaise, set aside.
Mix together sweet chili sauce and remaining 1/4 cup (60 ml) mayonnaise, set aside.
Assemble the sushi ginger, red peppers, cucumber, avocado, sprouts and green onions on serving platter and sprinkle with sesame seeds.
Brush fish with a bit of vegetable oil and grill until desired doneness. We like the tuna seared but still quite rare.
Slice the fish into thin slices and place on a platter. Serve with the warm rice.
Set the table with all the sushi ingredients and the sauces, and let everyone make their own rolls.

Experiment with different types of fish, vegetables and sauces. Prawns, scallops or even teriyaki beef would be delicious. Let the kids come up with their own signature roll. Next time you're dining at your local sushi bar, pick up some new ideas.

SHERI'S SOLE GRATIN WITH TOMATOES, CAPERS AND OLIVES

The lovely and talented Sheri Weichel really knows how to get a lot done in a day and still whip up a healthy delicious dinner for her adorable family. Most of the ingredients for this recipe can usually be found in your cupboards (except the fish of course). This is quick enough for a workday dinner, and its savoury aroma will fill the air.

- SERVES 4 -

INGREDIENTS

1 1/2 lbs (800 g) fresh sole, or red snapper

1 tsp (5 ml) salt

1 tsp (5 ml) pepper

1-28 oz (796 ml) can plum tomatoes, drained and chopped

1/3 cup (75 ml) olive oil

1 small onion, diced

1/4 cup (60 ml) pitted calamata olives, chopped

1 tbsp (15 ml) capers, drained

1/2 cup (125 ml) dried breadcrumbs, or panko crumbs

1/2 cup (125 ml) flat leaf parsley, chopped

2 tbsp (30 ml) olive oil

METHOD

Preheat oven to 400°F (200°C).

Lightly oil an oval gratin dish.

Season the fillets with salt and pepper, roll them up and place in the gratin dish.

Combine the tomatoes, olive oil, onion, olives, capers and 1/4 cup (60 ml) of the parsley.

Spoon the tomato mixture over the fish.

Combine the breadcrumbs, parsley and the 2 tbsp (30 ml) olive oil. Scatter the crumb mixture over the fish and place in the oven.

Cook for about 25 minutes until the breadcrumbs are crispy and brown and the fish is cooked through.

We love to serve fish on a bed of creamy mashed potatoes; it's light and fancy comfort food! This would be equally good with some steamed rice.

FILO WRAPPED SALMON WITH SAFFRON GINGER SAUCE

This is a perfect dish to prepare for small dinner parties. It may seem like a bit of work at first, but once your bundles of fish and savoury vegetables are all wrapped up you can relax. This deliciously creamy, golden hued sauce is a snap to prepare and is sure to become one of your favourites.

- SERVES 4 -

SAFFRON GINGER SAUCE

2 cups (500 ml) fish stock, or 1 cup (250 ml) clam nectar and 1 cup (250 ml) water
1 large shallot, finely chopped
2 tsp (10 ml) fresh ginger, finely chopped
2 garlic cloves, crushed
1 cup (250 ml) white wine
1 tsp (5 ml) fresh thyme, finely chopped
1 tbsp (15 ml) lobster paste or tomato paste
1 cup (250 ml) whipping cream
1/2 tsp (2 ml) saffron threads
juice of 1/2 a lemon
1 tbsp (15 ml) fresh dill, chopped

SALMON BUNDLES

2 lbs (about 1kg) skinless wild, fresh salmon fillets, cut into 6 serving sized pieces
2 tbsp (30 ml) olive oil
1 tbsp (15 ml) butter
3 large leeks, the white and a bit of the green, washed and diced
1/2 tsp (2 ml) salt
1/2 tsp (2 ml) pepper
2 bunches swiss chard, washed and roughly chopped
1/2 cup (125 ml) fresh dill, chopped
juice and zest of 1 lemon
salt and pepper
12 sheets filo pastry, thawed
1/2 cup (125 ml) butter, melted

METHOD

Combine the stock or clam nectar and water, shallot, ginger, garlic, wine and fresh thyme in a medium sized pot. Bring this mixture to a boil and reduce by half.
Pour through a fine mesh strainer, throw away the bits and return to the pot.
Add the lobster (or tomato paste), cream and saffron.
Simmer until thick, about 20 minutes.
Add lemon juice and dill and set aside until salmon is cooked.

Heat the olive oil and butter in a large pan and add the leeks, salt and pepper. Sauté for about 10 minutes until the leeks are softened.
Blanch the swiss chard in a large pot of boiling water for about 3 minutes. Drain and plunge into cold water, then drain and squeeze out all excess water.
Take 1 sheet of filo pastry and lay it on your work surface with the short end facing you. Brush it all over with some of the melted butter. Place another sheet of filo on top and brush it with butter.
Place 1 piece of salmon on the filo about 3 inches from the bottom, lengthwise. Put some of the swiss chard on top of it, then some of the leeks. Sprinkle with some of the fresh dill and lemon juice and zest.
Fold the left side of the filo dough over the fish towards the center to cover the fish. Do the same for the right side and then roll the bottom up toward the top. Keep rolling to make a nice snug bundle. Place on a

parchment paper lined baking sheet and brush some butter on the top. Continue with the remaining fish and vegetables until you have 6 packages.

Put the tray of filo bundles in the fridge until ready to bake.

Preheat oven to 400°F (200°C).

Bake for about 20 minutes until the filo is golden brown.

Serve with the Saffron Ginger Sauce.

Keep the salmon bundles in the fridge until just before serving. They can also be made well in advance and frozen uncooked. When cooking from frozen, place them on a baking sheet straight from the freezer and bake at 400°F (200°C) for about 30 minutes.

HURF'S HALIBUT

We started making halibut this way the day the fish truck delivered a whole 30 lb halibut to the catering truck (head, tail, eyes and all) one hour before we had to feed a film crew of 125 people. Jim Hurford, key grip and fisherman, came to our rescue. Not only did he fillet the fish into beautiful pieces in no time, he also told us how to cook it. This is his simple and sublime recipe for baked halibut. Thanks Hurf, wherever you are.

- SERVES 6 -

INGREDIENTS

2 1/2 lbs (1.25 kg) halibut fillet
1 cup (250 ml) mayonnaise
juice and zest of 1 lime
1 tbsp (15 ml) fresh ginger, finely chopped
1 small jalapeno pepper, seeded and finely chopped
1 tsp (5 ml) black pepper

METHOD

Preheat oven to 400°F (200°C).
Cut halibut into 6 equal pieces.
Combine mayonnaise, lime juice and zest, ginger, jalapeno and pepper together in small bowl.
Spread mayonnaise mixture evenly on to the top of each piece of halibut.
Bake in 400°F (200°C) oven for 15 to 20 minutes, depending on its thickness. The fish will be opaque and flaky when done.

Basmati rice and lightly steamed, fresh vegetables would be a great pairing for this ridiculously easy preparation.

SALMON WITH HERB BUTTER AND BROWN RICE PILAF

We've been eating this yummy salmon dinner for years and years. This unusual combination of herbs, butter and soy works surprisingly well together. We've served this countless times to movie crews over the years and always to rave reviews.

- SERVES 4 -

INGREDIENTS

1 salmon fillet, skin off (about 1 $^1/_2$ lbs or 800 g)
$^1/_2$ cup (125 ml) butter
2 tbsp (30 ml) japanese soy sauce
1 tbsp (15 ml) tarragon, dried or fresh
1 tbsp (15 ml) basil, dried or fresh
1 tbsp (15 ml) rosemary, dried or fresh

BROWN RICE PILAF

2 cups (500 ml) brown rice, cooked
$^1/_4$ cup (60 ml) butter
1 onion, diced
4 stalks celery, diced
1 cup (250 ml) slivered almonds, toasted
$^1/_2$ cup (125 ml) sour cream
$^1/_2$ cup (125 ml) parmesan
$^1/_2$ cup (125 ml) white wine
2 tbsp (30 ml) fresh parsley, chopped
1 tsp (5 ml) black pepper
1 tsp (5 ml) dried thyme
1 tbsp (15 ml) japanese soy sauce

METHOD

Melt butter in a small saucepan, then add soy sauce, tarragon, basil and rosemary. Remove from heat and let cool slightly.
Place salmon in a glass or ceramic dish and pour marinade over. Let the salmon marinate for about $^1/_2$ an hour.

Sauté onions and celery in $^1/_4$ cup (60 ml) melted butter until softened.
Place cooked brown rice in a large bowl and add sautéed onions and celery, toasted almonds, sour cream, parmesan, wine, parsley, pepper, thyme and soy sauce.
Mix well and place in an ovenproof dish. Put in a 350°F (180°C) oven for about 30 minutes or until thoroughly heated.
Preheat barbeque to medium high and spray with non-stick spray.
Place salmon on the barbeque and cook for approximately 10 minutes on each side or until the middle of the fillet is just starting to feel firm. Use 2 spatulas to flip the salmon.
Serve this salmon and pilaf with some lightly steamed vegetables.

We often serve this baked in the oven in the winter, and grilled in the summer. Either way, it's a great combination of flavours.

THAI CHICKEN ON THE BARBEQUE

Local caterer and chef Annie Bailey often barbeques huge amounts of this chicken at weddings and parties and her guests go wild. She is the fastest thing you have ever seen on two feet in a kitchen. She zooms!

- SERVES 8 -

INGREDIENTS

16 boneless skinless chicken thighs
1 can (400 ml) coconut milk
2 tbsp (30 ml) thai yellow curry paste*
8-10 kaffir lime leaves
1/4 cup (60 ml) fish sauce
6 garlic cloves, minced
1 tbsp (15 ml) fresh ginger, grated
1/2 tsp (2 ml) turmeric
2 tbsp (30 ml) sweet chili sauce
2 tbsp (30 ml) lemon grass, chopped finely
1 cup (250 ml) cilantro, chopped, for garnish
2 limes, quartered for garnish

METHOD

Combine coconut milk, curry paste, lime leaves, fish sauce, garlic, ginger, turmeric, sweet chili sauce and lemon grass in a large bowl.

Pour marinade over chicken in a large shallow baking dish. Cover and marinate overnight in the fridge.

Take the chicken out of the marinade. Cook on a medium barbeque for approximately 40 minutes moving them around so as not to burn. Flip them over once. You could also cook these in a 350°F (180°C) oven for 40 minutes.

Garnish with lots of chopped fresh cilantro and limes, and serve with extra sweet chili sauce on the side.

*Thai yellow curry paste can be found at Ellison's Market.

Thai Chicken just calls out for a pile of our Pad Thai Fried Noodles; the recipe can be found in Whitewatercooks #1.

SUMMERTIME PASTA WITH CHERRY TOMATOES, BASIL AND FRESH PARMESAN

This almost seems too simple, but in the summertime when tomatoes are at their juiciest and your basil plants are overproducing, this recipe is a very handy thing. Make the tomato mixture early in the day as it's even better if it sits at room temperature for a few hours.

- SERVES 6 -

INGREDIENTS

¹/₂ cup (125 ml) olive oil

6 garlic cloves, crushed

1 basket cherry tomatoes cut in half or 2 cups (500 ml) chopped fresh tomatoes

2 tsp (10 ml) sea salt

1 tsp (5 ml) black pepper

2 cups (500 ml) fresh basil, chopped

1 cup (250 ml) parmesan cheese, freshly grated

1 package (500 g) spaghetti or angel hair pasta

METHOD

Heat olive oil in frying pan over medium low heat and add garlic.

Cook just for a few seconds, mostly to infuse the oil with the garlic.

Transfer oil and garlic to a large bowl and add the tomatoes, salt, pepper and basil.

Cover and let the tomato mixture sit at room temperature for at least a few hours. We often do this step in the morning of the day we want to serve it.

Cook and drain the pasta.

Add the pasta to the tomato mixture and toss to combine.

Serve with freshly grated parmesan cheese.

We usually serve this pasta at room temperature after the warm pasta has soaked up all the goodness of the lovely tomato juices and garlicky olive oil. After you've made this a few times you'll start to improvise; goat cheese, asiago or a brie would all be fantastic additions.

We love roast chicken and we have to have it, even in the summertime when it's so hot that you can't bear to turn the oven on. Cooked whole on the barbeque, this chicken is wonderfully crisp and juicy because it's cooked slowly on low heat and flattened with tinfoil covered bricks or rocks. This is definitely the time to splurge on a nice, plump, organic chicken.

- SERVES 4 -

INGREDIENTS

1 whole chicken about 3 ½ lbs (1.75 kg)

juice of 4 lemons

1 tbsp (15 ml) lemon zest

¼ cup (60 ml) olive oil

1 tbsp (15 ml) fresh oregano, chopped

1 tbsp (15 ml) fresh rosemary, chopped

1 tsp (5 ml) smoked paprika (pimenton)

1 tsp (5 ml) pepper

1 tbsp (15 ml) coarse salt, divided

2 bricks or large flattish rocks covered with tinfoil

2 lemons for garnish

Of course this chicken can also be roasted in the oven for equally delicious flavour. Use the same method but cook in a 375°F (190°C) oven.

METHOD

Split the chicken by removing the backbone. Flip it over onto the breast so that the back is facing you. Use a sharp knife or sturdy kitchen scissors to cut through one side of the backbone. Now, cut along the other side of the backbone to remove it completely. Crack the breastbone with your knife so that the bird lies more or less flat.

Put the chicken in a baking dish or sealable container.

Combine the lemon juice, zest, olive oil, oregano, rosemary, smoked paprika (pimenton), pepper and 1 tsp (5 ml) salt.

Pour the mixture over the chicken and rub it in to coat completely. Cover and refrigerate for at least 4 hours, preferably overnight.

Preheat the barbeque to high heat for about 20 minutes (don't skip this part), then turn down to as low as your barbeque will go, 200°F (100°C) is perfect.

Take the chicken out of the marinade and sprinkle all over with the remaining 2 tsp (10 ml) salt.

Place the chicken on the barbeque skin side down. Place the foil covered bricks or rocks on top of the chicken to completely cover and flatten it.

Put the barbeque cover down and cook the chicken for about 40 minutes.

Remove the bricks and flip the chicken over, lifting slowly to avoid tearing the crispy skin.

Place back on the barbeque skin side up and cook for another 30 to 40 minutes. Check for doneness by poking a leg with a skewer. When juices are clear, it's ready.

ROAST LEG OF LAMB WITH CINZANO, ROSEMARY AND MINT DEMI-GLACE

The combination of cinzano, mint and red currant jelly makes a sauce that is fabulous with roast lamb. To us, it's all about the sauce! There are many good reasons to grow some mint in your garden and this is one of them.

- SERVES 6 TO 8 -

INGREDIENTS

one boneless leg of lamb, butterflied (about 5 lbs or 2.25 kg)

MARINADE

1 cup (250 ml) red wine
1/3 cup (75 ml) olive oil
3 cloves garlic, minced
2 tbsp (30 ml) dried oregano
1 tbsp (15 ml) fresh rosemary, chopped
1/4 cup (60 ml) fresh mint, chopped
1/4 cup (60 ml) dijon mustard
juice of 2 lemons

DEMI-GLACE

1/2 cup (125 ml) cinzano
1 cup (250 ml) demi-glace
1/3 cup (75 ml) red currant jelly
1 tbsp (15 ml) fresh rosemary, chopped
1/4 cup (60 ml) fresh mint, chopped

METHOD

Place lamb in a glass baking dish or in a heavy duty resealable bag. If the lamb has come wrapped in a net, cut it off.
Combine wine, olive oil, garlic, oregano, 1 tbsp (15 ml) rosemary, 1/4 cup (60 ml) mint, dijon, and the lemon juice. Pour over the lamb and cover with saran wrap or seal the bag. Let marinate overnight in fridge.
Preheat oven to 350°F (180°C).
Remove lamb from marinade and place in a roasting pan.
Roast lamb in 350°F (180°C) oven for approximately 1 hour. A meat thermometer inserted in the thickest part should read about 125°F (50°C).
Transfer lamb to platter and cover with tinfoil and let it rest for at least 20 minutes.

Combine the cinzano, demi-glace and red currant jelly and heat to simmering over medium heat. Simmer for 15 minutes. If you prefer a thicker sauce, mix together 1 tbsp (15 ml) cold butter and 1 tbsp (15 ml) flour and whisk in until incorporated.
Add the fresh rosemary and mint. You can also add any juices from the platter where the lamb has been resting.
Slice lamb and serve with the warm sauce.

This lamb is also fantastic cooked on the barbeque.
Our Roasted Red Potatoes with Pancetta and Red Peppers on Page 88 and a big fat greek salad would complete this dinner.

LING COD WITH TOMATO COCONUT CURRY

This is a deliciously light Indian curry that just makes the taste buds scream with happiness. Serve with basmati rice and a crispy pappadom on the side, if you like.

- SERVES 4 TO 6 -

INGREDIENTS

4 ling cod fillets (about 200 g each)
1/2 cup (125 ml) canola oil
12 kaffir lime leaves
1/2 tsp (2 ml) fenugreek seeds
2 tbsp (30 ml) garlic, minced
1 medium onion, finely chopped
4 medium tomatoes, diced
1 tbsp (15 ml) ground cumin
1 tbsp (15 ml) ground coriander
1/2 tsp (2 ml) turmeric
1 tsp (5 ml) salt
1/2 tsp (2 ml) cayenne pepper
1 cinnamon stick
1/2 tsp (2 ml) cloves
1 can (400 ml) coconut milk
1 cup (250 ml) fresh cilantro, chopped
salt and pepper to taste

METHOD

Heat oil in medium sized pot for 1 minute.
Add kaffir lime leaves and fenugreek seeds and allow them to sizzle for about 30 seconds. The leaves should shrivel a bit.
Add garlic and sauté for 3 to 4 minutes.
Add onions and sauté until light brown, about 10 minutes.
Stir in the tomatoes, cumin, coriander, turmeric, salt, cayenne, cinnamon stick and cloves. Continue cooking for about 10 minutes, or until the tomatoes have reduced a bit.
Add the coconut milk. Bring to a boil. Cover, turn heat down to medium low and simmer for about 20 minutes.

Place cod on a baking tray and sprinkle with salt and pepper.
Bake in 350°F (180°C) oven for about 15 minutes or until starting to flake.
Serve the fish with the curry over top, and garnish with the chopped cilantro.

This is a fantastic, versatile curry. Prawns or any firm texture white fish would be delicious with it. Beautiful, fresh fish is available at the Fisherman's Market Seafood & Deli, on Ward Street.

FLANK STEAK WITH SALSA VERDE

A flank steak is the busy cook's best friend. Marinated overnight and thrown on the barbeque to eat with a beautiful summer salad and some steamed new potatoes...nothing could be more delicious or require less effort.

- SERVES 4 -

INGREDIENTS

one flank steak (about 2 lbs or 1 kg)

MARINADE

1/4 cup (60 ml) soy sauce
1/4 cup (60 ml) red wine or 2 tbsp (30 ml) red wine vinegar
1/4 cup (60 ml) olive oil
1 tbsp (15 ml) honey or brown sugar
2 large cloves garlic, chopped
1 tbsp (15 ml) fresh thyme, chopped
1 tsp (5 ml) dried oregano
1 tsp (5 ml) black pepper, freshly ground

SALSA VERDE

2 tbsp (30 ml) capers, drained
2 tbsp (30 ml) shallot or red onion, chopped
3 anchovy fillets, finely chopped
1 garlic clove, crushed
1/2 cup (125 ml) fresh flat leaf parsley
1/2 cup (125 ml) fresh mint, basil or cilantro, or a combination
1 tsp (5 ml) dijon mustard
juice and zest of half a lemon
1 tsp (5 ml) pepper
1 tsp (5 ml) salt
1/3 cup (75 ml) olive oil

METHOD

Mix together all marinade ingredients. Pour over the steak in a sealable container or large zip lock bag.
This is best done the day before or in the morning of the day you want to cook it.
Make the Salsa Verde by combining capers, shallots, anchovies, garlic, fresh herbs, dijon, lemon juice and zest, pepper, salt and oil in a food processor and pulse until just blended. The texture should be a bit chunky. Make it ahead and refrigerate until needed. You could also hand chop the capers, shallots, anchovies, garlic and herbs together on a board then put in a bowl and stir in the remaining ingredients.

Preheat the barbeque to high heat. Lightly oil the grill.
Remove the steak from the marinade. Turn the barbeque down to medium and grill the steak for about 5 to 7 minutes per side. Let it rest, covered for at least 10 minutes and up to 1/2 hour before slicing.
Slice steak diagonally across the grain and as thinly as you can.
Place the sliced steak on a platter and pour any juices from carving over the meat.
Serve topped with a spoonful of the Salsa Verde.

Salsa Verde is such a fantastic little sauce; it's light, fresh and super easy. It's also great served with any type of fresh fish or a grilled chicken breast.

FENNEL INFUSED PORK RIB ROAST

Serve this when you have a busy day but still want to give your guests something impressive. This gorgeous roast is placed on top of a bed of fennel and onions so the juices and flavours are infused into the pork while marinating and roasting.

- SERVES 6 TO 8 -

INGREDIENTS

one pork loin roast, bone in (about 4 lbs or 2 kg)
4 garlic cloves, peeled and sliced in half
2 fennel bulbs, thinly sliced
2 large onions, thinly sliced
2 cups (500 ml) white wine
juice and zest of 1 large orange
1 tbsp (15 ml) fresh rosemary, chopped
2 tsp (10 ml) fresh thyme, chopped
2 tbsp (30 ml) dijon mustard
1 tbsp (15 ml) olive oil
1 tsp (5 ml) salt
1 tsp (5 ml) pepper

METHOD

Pierce pork with a knife and insert garlic slices in meat.
Place fennel, onion slices, wine, orange juice and zest, rosemary and thyme in the bottom of a large roasting pan.
Place pork on top of the fennel and onion mixture and let marinate covered in the fridge for up to 4 hours, turning a few times.
Remove the roast from the fridge and rub the top of the pork with the dijon and olive oil. Sprinkle with the salt and pepper.
Roast in 350°F (180°C) oven for 1 hour and 20 minutes.
Remove, let rest for at least 15 minutes then slice and serve with the braised fennel and onions on the side.

Pair this with some mashed potatoes and our Warm Red Cabbage Salad on Page 54 for a dinner that is relaxing for both cook and guests.

RYAN'S MOROCCAN YAM BURGERS

Thanks to Ryan Zsdany for sharing this delicious veggie burger rendition. Ryan is one of the many talented chefs that shared his expertise and enthusiasm in the Whitewater kitchen over the years. A food processor really does come in handy for this one.

- MAKES 12 PATTIES -

INGREDIENTS

6 cups (1.5 L) grated yams (about 2 lbs or 1 kg)
2 tbsp (30 ml) garlic, peeled and coarsely chopped
2 tbsp (30 ml) ginger, peeled and coarsely chopped
1-19 oz (540 ml) can chickpeas, rinsed and drained
1 1/2 cups (375 ml) unsalted mixed nuts
1/2 cup (125 ml) fresh cilantro, chopped
2 tsp (10 ml) cumin
1 tbsp (15 ml) chili powder
1 tsp (5 ml) coriander
1/2 tsp (2 ml) cinnamon
1tsp (5 ml) pepper
2 tbsp (30 ml) soy sauce
2 tbsp (30 ml) sesame oil
1 tbsp (15 ml) egg replacer powder mixed with
3 tbsp (45 ml) water (or 2 eggs)
1/3 cup (75 ml) dry breadcrumbs
vegetable oil for sautéing

METHOD

Peel the yams and grate them in a food processor or by hand. Remove to a large bowl.
Put the garlic and ginger in the food processor and pulse until finely chopped.
Add half of the chickpeas to garlic and ginger and process until fairly smooth. Add this mixture to the shredded yams.
Put the remaining chickpeas in a bowl and mash them slightly with a potato masher or a large metal spoon.
Add them to the yam mixture.
Add nuts to food processor and grind until coarsely chopped. Add them to the yam mixture.
Add cilantro, cumin, chili powder, coriander, cinnamon and black pepper to the yam mixture and mix well.
Mix the egg powder mixture, or eggs, in a small bowl, set aside.
Add soy sauce and sesame oil to the yam mixture and mix well.
Add eggs or egg replacer and breadcrumbs. You may need a bit more breadcrumbs. Measure into half-cup portions and form into patties.
Sauté on medium low, approximately 5 minutes on each side.
Serve on a whole wheat bun with lettuce, tomato, sliced red onions and tzatziki.

This recipe makes a lot of burger patties, but they are great to have in the freezer when you have a vegan or two in your crowd.

DESSERTS

FILO CUPS WITH SAUTÉED BANANAS AND CARAMEL SAUCE

The tulip shaped cups are crispy and light and appear fancy, as if you went to a lot of work. Only you will know that you didn't.

- SERVES 6 -

FILO CUPS

4 sheets filo dough
1/4 cup (60 ml) melted butter
3 tbsp (45 ml) sugar
1 tsp (5 ml) cinnamon

CARAMEL SAUCE

1/4 cup (60 ml) butter
1/2 cup (125 ml) brown sugar
1/2 cup (125 ml) whipping cream

SAUTEED BANANAS

6 bananas
1/4 cup (60 ml) butter
1/4 cup (60 ml) brown sugar
1/4 cup (60 ml) dark rum, orange liqueur,
or orange juice
6 scoops vanilla ice cream

METHOD - CARAMEL SAUCE

Melt the butter over medium high heat and then add brown sugar and simmer on low for 5 minutes until completely incorporated, stirring constantly.
Add the whip cream and let cook, still on low, for another 5 minutes, gently whisking constantly. Keep warm or reheat when you are ready to use.

METHOD - FILO CUPS

Preheat oven to 350°F (180°C).
Combine the sugar and cinnamon in a small bowl.
Lay one sheet of filo pastry on the countertop and brush with melted butter.
Sprinkle with a bit of the sugar cinnamon mixture.
Carry on with 3 more sheets, buttering and sprinkling with cinnamon sugar between sheets. You will have a stack of 4 sheets. Roll the stacked sheets a little with a rolling pin to help them stick together a bit.
Brush muffin tins with a little melted butter.
Cut stacked sheets into 12 squares 3 lengthwise and 4 widthwise.
Press each square into a muffin hole and make a little cup, making sure to push the filo gently right into the bottom.
Bake for 15 minutes, or until golden brown and crisp.
Let cool in pans and then transfer to a cooling rack, or a storage container if not using right away.

METHOD - SAUTÉED BANANAS

Slice bananas. Heat the butter in a large sauté pan until melted, keeping on medium high heat.
Sauté the bananas until slightly brown.
Add the brown sugar and sauté until sugar melts and coats the bananas.
Add the rum, orange liqueur or orange juice and give the pan a shake. Ignite the rum (if using) and either wait until the flames subside or blow them out (be careful!).
Serve by placing each filo cup on a dessert plate and fill with a scoop of vanilla ice cream. Top with warm bananas and drizzle with caramel sauce.

For some variety use pineapple or peaches in place of the bananas. Try grilling the fruit - it's a nice alternative to sautéing, especially in the summer when the barbeque is handy and the peaches are ripe.

MARIANNE'S CHOCOLATE BASIL CREME BRULEE

If you feel like showing off a little, this sublime chocolate creme brulee with the added twist of basil infused cream may be just what you're looking for.

- SERVES 8 -

INGREDIENTS

2 cups (500 ml) whipping cream
1/4 cup (60 ml) milk
1/2 cup (125 ml) fresh basil leaves
4 oz (125 g) good quality dark chocolate, chopped in small pieces
2 whole eggs
4 egg yolks
3/4 cup (175 ml) sugar

*If you own a small kitchen blowtorch, use it to melt and caramelize the sugar.

When you use egg yolks only in a recipe, freeze surplus egg whites in a little plastic bag for other uses. Four egg whites are just the right amount for our Meringue recipe on Page 138.

Substituting fresh mint for the basil is absolutely delicious.

METHOD

Preheat oven to 325°F (160°C).
Infuse cream with the fresh basil leaves by heating cream, milk and basil over minimum heat until liquid has reached scalding point, about 15 minutes. Do not boil.
Place the chopped chocolate in a medium sized mixing bowl.
Strain the infused cream to remove all the basil. Pour the hot cream mixture over the chopped chocolate and let sit for a minute or two.
Stir chocolate and cream mixture until completely incorporated with no lumps.
Combine the eggs, egg yolks and sugar together in a large bowl. Whisk until pale yellow and slightly thickened. Continue mixing and slowly drizzle warm chocolate cream mixture into the egg mixture. Whisk until incorporated.
Fill 8 ovenproof ramekins to 3/4 full. Place in a shallow baking pan and fill with hot water to about halfway up the ramekins.
Bake until just set, about 45 minutes or until they no longer jiggle.
Cool completely, then refrigerate for at least a few hours and up to overnight.
Sprinkle the tops of each creme brulee with 1 tsp (5 ml) of white or light brown sugar. Do this just before serving.
Place ramekins on a baking sheet and broil* for 1 minute until the sugar begins to melt and bubble. Watch closely. Once it cools off, the sugar will harden, forming a crisp sugary crust that's just waiting for the tap, tap of your spoon.

MERINGUES WITH RASPBERRIES, PEACHES AND CREAM

Light and airy, sweet and fruity, these are always a crowd pleaser and it's easy to understand why. We like serving them in the summer because meringues bake better on dry days and because that's when all of our fabulous local fruit is in season.

- SERVES 8 -

INGREDIENTS

4 egg whites, room temperature
pinch (1 ml) of salt
1 cup (250 ml) sugar
1 tsp (5 ml) cornstarch
1 tsp (5 ml) lemon juice

1 1/2 cups (375 ml) whipping cream
1/4 cup (60 ml) sour cream
3 tbsp (45 ml) icing sugar
2 tsp (10 ml) pure vanilla extract
2 cups (500 ml) fresh raspberries
2 or 3 fresh peaches, peeled and sliced

METHOD

Preheat oven to 225°F (105°C).

Make 8 approximately 4 inch (10 cm) circles on 2 sheets of parchment paper by tracing a glass or cookie cutter with a pencil or pen. Flip the paper circles over and place them on 2 baking sheets.

Whip the egg whites and salt until frothy on medium high.

Start adding the sugar 1/4 cup (60 ml) at a time and keep beating until the egg whites form stiff peaks and all the sugar is added. Gently fold in the cornstarch and lemon juice.

Spread the meringue onto the traced circles making a little nest shape with the back of a spoon.

Bake for about an hour and a half. You don't want the meringues to brown at all so check them at 20 minutes and turn the oven down if necessary. When done they should be dry and crisp and easy to remove from the parchment paper.

Cool on a rack.

Whip cream for a minute or two then add sour cream, icing sugar and vanilla. Whip to soft peaks.

Assemble the meringues on a big platter or individual plates. Pile the tops up with the cream and then the fruit. You can give them a little dusting of icing sugar if you like.

The sky is the limit when it comes to fruit for topping the meringues, as just about any fruit or berry combination works beautifully. The meringues can also be made a day or two ahead and kept in an airtight container at room temperature.

PISTACHIO AND POLENTA BISCOTTI

We love these biscotti. They are full of flavour and have a unique texture because of the cornmeal. Serve them after dinner with a glass of vin santo or port to soften them and accentuate their flavour. Before travelling to Italy, we thought biscotti was always served with cappuccino, but pair them with a sweet wine for an authentic treat.

- MAKES 24 -

INGREDIENTS

1/4 cup (60 ml) butter, softened
1/2 cup (125 ml) sugar
1 egg, lightly beaten
2 tsp (10 ml) brandy or orange flavoured liqueur
zest of 1 lemon
1 1/2 cups (375 ml) all purpose flour
1/4 tsp (2 ml) salt
2 tsp (10 ml) baking powder
1 tsp (5 ml) ground coriander
1/2 cup (125 ml) cornmeal
1/2 cup (125 ml) whole almonds, roughly chopped
1/2 cup (125 ml) unsalted pistachio nuts, roughly chopped

METHOD

Preheat oven to 325°F (160°C).
Prepare a baking sheet by lining with parchment paper.
Cream together the butter and sugar until light and fluffy.
Add the egg, brandy or orange flavoured liqueur and lemon zest, beating well to incorporate.
Sift or whisk together the flour, salt, baking powder, coriander and cornmeal.
Fold together the egg mixture and the flour mixture to make a soft dough.
Stir in the almonds and pistachio nuts until evenly combined.
Divide the mixture into 2 halves.
Shape each half into a flat log about 9 inches (22.5 cm) long.
Bake for about 30 minutes until risen and just firm.
Remove from oven and set pan on cooling rack and let cool for about 20 minutes. Slide log off the baking sheet onto a cutting board. Cut each log diagonally into 12 slices.
Return to the baking sheet and bake for a further 15 to 20 minutes until crisp and golden brown.
Transfer to a rack to cool completely. Store in an airtight tin or a jar for up to 2 weeks.

Using a sharp serrated knife will make slicing the cooled biscotti much easier and avoid crumbling. Chocolate lovers may want to dip the baked and cooled biscotti in melted white or dark chocolate.

BLUEBERRY ALMOND BARS

We're supposed to eat lots of blueberries and almonds because they're so darn good for us.
Here's a scrumptious way to do it.

- MAKES 12 BIG BARS -

INGREDIENTS

1 1/2 cups (375 ml) butter, room temperature
1 1/2 cups (375 ml) brown sugar
2 cups (500 ml) rolled oats
1 1/2 cups (375 ml) flour
1 cup (250 ml) sliced almonds
1 tsp (5 ml) baking powder
1/2 tsp (2 ml) salt
1 1/2 tsp (7 ml) cinnamon

4 cups (1 kg) blueberries fresh or frozen (if using frozen do not thaw)
3/4 cup (175 ml) sugar
1 tsp (5 ml) almond extract
1/4 tsp (1 ml) freshly ground nutmeg
2 tbsp (30 ml) flour

METHOD

Preheat the oven to 350°F (180°C).
Prepare a 9x13 inch (23x28 cm) baking pan by greasing and lining with parchment paper or foil to come up the sides of the pan. This will make it easier to remove the bars.
Beat together the butter and brown sugar until light and fluffy.
Add the rest of the crust ingredients and mix until combined and crumbly.
Press 2/3 of the crust mixture firmly into the pan with your fingers.

Toss the blueberry filling ingredients together and spread them over the bottom crust.
Sprinkle the remaining crust on top, pressing gently. The blueberries should be almost completely covered.
Bake for about 40 minutes until light golden brown.
Cool completely before cutting.

Try other types of fruit for some variety, rhubarb or raspberries would be good. These bars freeze well and make a great alternative to store bought backpack snacks.

ENERGY BALLS

Up the mountain these sell like crazy to the touring crowd heading up for a day of carbo burning adventure. For home consumption or the lunchbox you may want to make these a little smaller.

- MAKES ABOUT 20 -

INGREDIENTS

1 cup (250 ml) sunflower seeds, toasted
1 cup (250 ml) sesame seeds, toasted
1 cup (250 ml) rolled oats
1 cup (250 ml) chocolate chips
1 cup (250 ml) raisins
1 cup (250 ml) dried cranberries
1/2 cup (125 ml) cocoa powder
2 cups (500 ml) peanut butter
1/2 cup (125 ml) honey
1 1/2 cups (375 ml) toasted coconut (for coating)

METHOD

Put everything except coconut in a large bowl.
Mix all ingredients together well with your hands. You may need a bit more honey to hold it together.
Roll 1/4 cup (60 ml) scoops of dough into balls and then roll them in the toasted coconut.

Store the energy balls in an airtight container in the fridge for up to one week or the freezer for a couple of months.

You can easily get creative with the dried fruit in this recipe, just use your favourite combinations.

DAD'S LUNCHBOX COOKIES

Another one of Gail's terrific family cookie recipes. A favourite of her dad's, and dads everywhere.

- MAKES 18 COOKIES -

INGREDIENTS

1 cup (250 ml) butter, room temperature
1 cup (250 ml) white sugar
1/2 cup (125 ml) brown sugar
1 egg
1 tsp (5 ml) vanilla
1 1/2 cups (375 ml) flour
1/2 tsp (2 ml) cinnamon
1 tsp (5 ml) baking soda
1 tsp (5 ml) baking powder
1 1/2 cups (375 ml) rolled oats
3/4 cup (175 ml) coconut
1 cup (250 ml) white chocolate chunks
1 cup (250 ml) raisins, dried cranberries,
dried blueberries, or a combination.

METHOD

Preheat oven to 350°F (180°C).
Line 2 cookie sheets with parchment paper.
Cream the butter with both sugars until light and fluffy.
Add egg and vanilla and mix to combine.
Sift together flour, cinnamon, baking soda and baking powder, and beat into the butter mixture.
Stir in the oats, coconut, white chocolate and your chosen combination of the fruit.
Drop by spoonful onto prepared pan.
Bake for about 12 minutes. Do not overbake because they are meant to be a bit chewy.
Cool on a rack and store in a cookie tin.

A 1 1/2 inch spring loaded scoop is a really handy thing to have for cookie baking. All your cookies will be the same size and shape and will bake evenly and perfectly.

LIME YOGURT PANNA COTTA

A wonderful balance of creamy and tart flavours, this makes a fantastic summertime dessert. It's light and super easy. Don't be intimidated by gelatin, once you get the hang of it you'll never look back.

- SERVES 6 -

INGREDIENTS

1 cup (250 ml) full fat natural yogurt*
1/4 cup (60 ml) fresh lime juice
2 tsp (10 ml) lime zest
1 tsp (5 ml) unflavoured gelatin powder
1 1/4 cups (300 ml) whipping cream, divided
1/2 cup (125 ml) sugar
lime zest for garnish

*You can only make yogurt cheese from yogurt that does not contain any thickening agents, such as those found in some non-fat products. Yogurt cheese is delicious and can be used to make all kinds of dips and sauces.

METHOD

Line a fine mesh strainer with a couple of pieces of paper towel.
Put the yogurt in the strainer and place it over a bowl. Cover and put it into the refrigerator for a few hours or overnight. The liquid will drain out of the yogurt leaving you with a lovely thick yogurt cheese.
Combine 1/4 cup (60 ml) lime juice and zest in small saucepan; sprinkle gelatin over and let soften for 5 minutes.
Add 1/4 cup (60 ml) of the whipping cream to gelatin mixture. Stir over low heat just until gelatin dissolves. Remove from heat.
Whisk yogurt cheese and 1/2 cup (125 ml) sugar in medium bowl. Gradually whisk in remaining 1 cup (250 ml) whipping cream until smooth.
Whisk gelatin mixture into cream mixture until combined.
Pour and spoon into any pretty little glasses or ramekins that you have. We like to use little white chinese tea bowls (inexpensive and easy to store in the fridge). Cover with plastic wrap and chill until set, at least 4 hours or overnight.
Serve alone or topped with lime zest, fresh raspberries or mango.

POACHED PEAR AND FRANGIPANE TART

This is best in the fall when local pears are perfect. If you poach the pears and make the frangipane and cornmeal dough the day ahead, you'll only have to assemble and bake the tarts before serving. Try drizzling these beautiful tarts with some melted dark chocolate.

- MAKES TWO TARTS, SERVES 10 TO 12 -

INGREDIENTS

1 recipe Cornmeal Dough (Page 20)

POACHED PEARS

3 cups (750 ml) white wine
2 tbsp (30 ml) lemon juice
1 cup (250 ml) sugar
1 cinnamon stick
zest of 1 lemon
6 whole, firm but ripe pears, peeled with stems on

FRANGIPANE

1/2 cup (125 ml) butter, room temperature
1/2 cup (125 ml) sugar
1 egg
1 cup (250 ml) almonds, toasted and coarsely ground
3 tbsp (45 ml) dark rum or brandy (or 1 tbsp (15 ml) vanilla extract)
1 tsp (5 ml) almond extract
1 tbsp (15 ml) flour

METHOD

Combine wine, lemon juice, sugar, cinnamon stick and lemon zest in large pot.
Bring the mixture to a boil, then lower the heat until simmering.
Add the peeled pears and simmer gently for about 20 to 30 minutes until tender. You may need to turn them occasionally by rotating the stems.
Remove the pears to a bowl and pour the poaching liquid over them.
Cover the bowl with saran wrap and refrigerate for at least 2 hours or overnight.
Remove pears from the poaching liquid and place in a bowl.
Pour poaching liquid into a saucepan and reduce over medium heat until syrupy. This will be used to glaze the finished tart.
Cut each pear in half, removing stems and cores.

Make the frangipane by creaming the butter and sugar until light and fluffy.
Add the egg, almonds, rum, almond extract and flour and beat until smooth. Refrigerate for about 15 minutes to firm it up a bit.

Roll out the cornmeal dough into 11 inch (28 cm) rounds on a flour dusted surface.
Place dough on 2 parchment paper lined baking trays.
Spread frangipane on dough in a thin layer in the middle, leaving edges free for folding around the pears.
Place the pears on the frangipane and press in gently. Make slices in the pears so that they fan open a bit.
Fold the edges of the tart up and over to form small folds along the edge of the dough. Press gently to adhere.
Bake at 375°F (190°C) for 45 minutes, or until the pastry is golden brown and the frangipane has puffed and browned.
Brush some of the reserved poaching syrup on tarts while they are still warm. Serve with whipped cream.

MANGO COCONUT BREAD PUDDING

We actually love bread pudding for breakfast! But of course it's an excellent dessert, especially
if paired with a light dinner menu.

- SERVES 8 -

INGREDIENTS

2 tbsp (30 ml) butter
1 cup (250 ml) milk
1/4 cup (60 ml) honey
1 tsp (5 ml) vanilla (or dark rum)
1 can (400 ml) coconut milk
3 large eggs
6 cups (1.5 kg) day old french bread or challah, cubed
2 cups (500 ml) ripe mango, peeled and diced
1/3 cup (75 ml) shredded coconut, toasted

1/2 cup (125 ml) sugar
1 cup (250 ml) apricot or mango nectar
2 cups (500 ml) good quality yogurt

METHOD

Prepare a 9x11 inch (23x28 cm) glass baking dish by
greasing with the butter.
Combine milk, honey, vanilla, coconut milk and eggs in
a large bowl, and mix well.
Stir in cubed bread and mango and let sit at room
temperature for half an hour.
Preheat oven to 350°F (180°C).
Pour mixture into the prepared baking dish. Bake for
1 hour, then sprinkle with the toasted coconut and bake
for another 10 minutes.
Remove from oven and let rest for half an hour.

Combine sugar and nectar in a small pan. Bring to a
boil, reduce heat, and simmer for 10 minutes until syrupy.
Cool to room temperature.
Add the yogurt and stir well to combine.
Serve by scooping the bread pudding into bowls. Dollop
with some of the yogurt sauce.

If you would prefer a warm, slightly richer sauce with your bread pudding try it with a custard or crème anglaise.

TRES LECHE CAKE

This is another delicious recipe from our lovely friend Linda Klein. She was in Mexico recently at a big family wedding where she was introduced to this moist and unusual cake. The three different kinds of milk added after baking the cake may sound odd to us but it's traditional. Everything Linda creates is perfect and this is no exception.

- SERVES 8 TO 10 -

INGREDIENTS

6 eggs, separated
1 1/4 cups (300 ml) sugar, divided
1/2 cup (125 ml) milk
1 tsp (5 ml) vanilla
2 tbsp (30 ml) finely grated lemon zest
2 cups (500 ml) flour
2 tsp (10 ml) baking powder
1 can (370 ml) evaporated milk
1 can (300 ml) sweetened condensed milk
1/2 cup (125 ml) half and half cream
4 cups (1 L) fresh fruit
2 cups (500 ml) whipping cream
1 tbsp (15 ml) sugar
1/2 tsp (2 ml) cinnamon

METHOD

Preheat oven to 350°F (180°C).
Prepare a 9x13 inch (22x27 cm) pan or a 12 inch (30 cm) round cake pan by greasing.
Beat the egg yolks with 3/4 cup (175 ml) of the sugar until light in colour and doubled in volume.
Stir in the milk, vanilla, lemon zest, flour and baking powder.
Beat the egg whites until soft peaks form, gradually adding the remaining 1/2 cup (125 ml) sugar. Continue beating until firm but not dry.
Fold egg whites into the yolk mixture. Pour batter into prepared pan.
Bake at 350°F (180°C) for about 40 minutes or until a skewer comes out clean.
Poke holes all over the cake with a wooden skewer.
Whisk together the evaporated milk, the condensed milk and the half and half. Pour evenly over the warm cake.
Cool cake to room temperature and chill in the fridge for a minimum of 4 hours.
Whip the cream and add the sugar and cinnamon.
Serve with the whipped cream and a bowl of your favorite fresh fruit combination.

We like to use mangoes, kiwis, papaya and blackberries but use any combination that you like. When layered with strawberries and whipped cream this cake makes for a wonderful twist on the traditional strawberry shortcake. Make a day or two ahead if you like, because this cake improves as the milk is absorbed.

CHOCOLATE CLEMENTINE CAKE

This cake has everything going for it; beautiful texture, sweet orangey aroma, fantastic flavour and versatility. You can eat this all by itself or gussied up with some sliced boozy oranges, caramel sauce and a little devon or whipped cream.

- SERVES 8 TO 10 -

INGREDIENTS

4 clementines (about 300 g)
2 cups (500 ml) finely ground almonds or almond flour
1/2 cup (125 ml) cocoa powder, packed
1 tsp (5 ml) baking powder
1/2 tsp (2 ml) baking soda
1/2 tsp (2 ml) salt
5 eggs
1 cup (250 ml) sugar

Clementines are relatively easy to find in the grocery store year round. They come from California and are often called "cuties". We like to cook up a whole bag then freeze 4 oranges at a time in small bags so that you can whip this wonderful cake up at a moment's notice.

METHOD

Put the unpeeled oranges in a pot and cover with water.
Bring to a boil and simmer gently for about an hour until they are soft.
Drain in a colander and cool completely.
Preheat oven to 350°F (180°C).
Prepare a 10x2.5 inch bundt pan (one of those flexible plastic ones works great for this) by greasing with butter. You can also use an 8 inch (20 cm) springform pan, just grease it and line the bottom with parchment paper.
Put the cooked and cooled oranges, (peel and all) into a food processor or blender and pulse until quite smooth.
Whisk together the ground almonds, cocoa powder, baking powder, baking soda and salt. Set aside.
Beat the eggs and sugar together in a large mixing bowl until well combined.
Add the dry ingredients and beat well.
Add the orange pulp and beat on low until just combined.
Pour into prepared pan.
Bake for 1 hour. A wooden skewer should come out fairly clean.
Cool for about 30 minutes before removing carefully from the pan.
Serve with a dollop of devon or whipped cream.

OLD FASHIONED BANANA CAKE

The icing on this cake sets it apart from other banana cakes. It's whipped, creamy and really complements this delicious old family cake recipe from the adoreable Emmy. It makes a great kid's birthday cake or lunchbox snack.

- SERVES 12 -

INGREDIENTS

1 cup (250 ml) butter, room temperature
2 cups (500 ml) sugar
4 eggs
4 large bananas, mashed
1 cup (250 ml) whole milk
2 tsp (10 ml) vinegar
1/2 cup (125 ml) warm water
2 tsp (10 ml) vanilla
2 tsp (10 ml) baking soda
4 cups (1 kg) flour
2 tsp (10 ml) baking powder
1/2 tsp (2 ml) salt
1 cup (250 ml) chopped walnuts

1 cup (250 ml) butter
2 cups (500 ml) icing sugar
2 tbsp (30 ml) boiling water
2 tbsp (30 ml) milk
1 tsp (5 ml) vanilla
1 cup (250 ml) toasted coconut

METHOD

Preheat oven to 350°F(180°).
Prepare two round 9 inch (22.5 cm) pans by greasing and lining the bottoms with parchment paper.

Combine butter and sugar and beat until light and fluffy in a large mixing bowl.
Add eggs one at a time, beating after each addition. Add mashed bananas and beat the batter until combined.
Combine the milk and vinegar in medium sized bowl or large measuring cup. Add warm water and vanilla. Stir in the baking soda. The mixture will fizz up a bit. Set aside.
Mix together the dry ingredients: flour, baking powder, and salt.
Add the dry ingredients to the batter in three parts, alternating with the milk mixture in two parts, mixing gently between each addition until just blended.
Fold in the walnuts.
Pour into prepared pans.
Bake for about 45 minutes or until a skewer or toothpick comes out clean.
Cool for 20 minutes before removing from the pan.

Cream butter and icing sugar until light and fluffy.
Add boiling water and beat well.
Beat in the milk and vanilla and whip for about 2 minutes until icing is light and fluffy.
Place toasted coconut onto a big pan.
Spread the icing on the cake between the layers (you may want to trim the top off the bottom layer to make it flat). Next, spread icing on the sides of the cake, leaving the top un-iced. With one hand on the bottom and one on the top of the cake, roll the sides into the toasted coconut. Then set the cake on a serving platter and finish by icing the top.

- 154 -

SUMMER CAKE WITH NECTARINES

It's a summer cake because almost any seasonal fruit will do and it's so quick and easy to pull together that you can whip it up without the slightest bit of stress. This makes it an essential addition to your summertime baking repertoire.

- SERVES 6 TO 8 -

INGREDIENTS

1 cup (250 ml) flour
1/4 cup (60 ml) cornmeal
1 tsp (5 ml) baking powder
1/2 tsp (2 ml) salt
1/2 cup (125 ml) butter
1 cup (250 ml) sugar
3 large eggs
1 tbsp (15 ml) lemon juice
zest of 1 lemon

3 firm but ripe nectarines
1 tbsp (15 ml) lemon juice
2 tbsp (30 ml) brown sugar
1 tbsp (15 ml) white sugar
1 tsp (5 ml) cinnamon

METHOD

Preheat oven to 350°F (180°C).

Prepare a 10 inch (22.5 cm) springform pan or an 8 inch (20 cm) square glass pan by greasing and lining the bottom with parchment paper.

Sift together the flour, cornmeal, baking powder and salt. Set aside.

Cream the butter and sugar together in a mixing bowl until light and fluffy. Beat in the eggs one at a time; add the lemon juice and zest.

Add the dry ingredients and mix until just combined.

Spread the batter evenly into your prepared cake pan.

Cut the nectarines in half and remove the pits. Cut each half into 6 wedges. Toss the fruit with 1 tbsp (15 ml) lemon juice.

Place the nectarines in a pretty pattern in your cake pan by starting at the outside of the cake and working around to the center. Place the fruit in rows if you are using a square pan.

Mix the sugars and cinnamon together and sprinkle on top of the cake.

Bake for 40 minutes until a wooden skewer comes out clean.

Cool completely before slicing.

This simple cake is great served with some good vanilla ice cream or lightly whipped cream.

TARTE AUX POMMES

This classic french tart is perfect for any time of the year. It looks so beautiful just sitting on
a pretty platter in your kitchen that it makes you feel good about your efforts, like you could
be a pastry chef in a Parisian bistro on Boulevard Saint-Michel.

- SERVES 8 -

INGREDIENTS

Makes enough dough for 2-9 inch
(22.5 cm) tart shells

2 1/2 cups (375 ml) flour
1 tsp (5 ml) salt
1 tsp (5 ml) sugar
1 cup (250 ml) butter, cold and cut into
small pieces
1/4 cup (60 ml) to 1/2 cup (125 ml) ice
water

4-6 firm apples (about 3 cups), peeled
and thinly sliced
1/3 cup (75 ml) sugar
1/2 tsp (2 ml) cinnamon
1 egg
1/3 cup (75 ml) sugar
1/4 cup (60 ml) flour
1/2 cup (125 ml) whipping cream
3 tbsp (45 ml) brandy or rum
2 tbsp (30 ml) icing sugar

Serve warm from the oven or room
temperature with whipped cream
flavoured with a pinch of cinnamon.

METHOD

Put the flour, salt and sugar in a food processor.
Add the pieces of butter and process for no longer than 10 seconds.
Add the ice water bit by bit with the food processor running, until pastry
just pulls together. Check it after you have added 1/4 cup (60 ml) of the
water. If it is still crumbly, add the rest of the water.
Remove the pastry and wrap in two rounds in plastic wrap. Refrigerate
for at least an hour or until ready to use. Keep one round in the freezer
for another time.
Preheat oven to 375°F (190°C).
Roll out pastry on a lightly floured work surface in a round. Lift it up and
place it into a 9 inch (22.5 cm) removable bottom tart pan. Fit in with
your fingers and press around the crimped edge of the pan to cut off
extra pastry. Prick pastry all around with a fork.
Bake for about 10 minutes, until partially baked.
Remove from the oven and place on a rack. Reduce oven
temperature to 350°F (180°C).

Toss apples with sugar and cinnamon.
Arrange apples in spiral layers around circumference of the shell until
you reach the middle.
Bake for 20 minutes until apples start to soften and shrink and look crisp
on the edges. Remove from the oven and set aside.
Beat the egg and sugar together until very thick and pale yellow in
colour. Add flour, cream and brandy or rum and mix until incorporated.
Pour the mixture over the apples, slowly and carefully, letting the liquid
settle into the pan and all around the apples. Return to the oven for 10
minutes until just starting to set.
Remove from the oven again and sprinkle with icing sugar. Return to
oven for 20 more minutes at 350°F (180°C). The tart will be beautifully
golden brown and set in the middle when done.

CAROLINE'S GINGERBREAD COOKIES

These are perfect for rolling out and decorating with the kids. If you poke a hole in the top of the cookie with a skewer just before baking you can string them up to hang on the Christmas tree. Just make sure your dog and the kids can handle the temptation or you might have trouble keeping the tree upright.

- MAKES ABOUT 4 DOZEN -

INGREDIENTS

4 cups (1 kg) flour
2 tbsp (30 ml) cocoa powder
2 tbsp (30 ml) ginger
2 tsp (10 ml) cinnamon
1 tsp (5 ml) cloves
1 tsp (5 ml) baking soda
1 tsp (5 ml) salt
1 cup (250 ml) butter, softened
1 cup (250 ml) sugar
1 egg, lightly beaten
1/2 cup (125 ml) molasses

METHOD

Sift together flour, cocoa, ginger, cinnamon, cloves, baking soda and salt in a medium sized bowl and set aside.
Cream the butter with the sugar until light and fluffy. Beat in the egg then gradually beat in the molasses. Slowly beat in the flour until just combined.
Turn dough out onto lightly floured surface and knead gently a few times.
Divide the dough into 4 pieces and flatten into disks. Wrap each piece in plastic wrap and refrigerate for at least 4 hours.
Preheat oven to 350°F (180°C).
Prepare two parchment lined baking sheets.
Roll dough out to desired thickness. We like them pretty thin but it depends on how big your cutters are. If little kids are handling them you may want to roll them a little thicker. Cut out shapes and place on baking sheet.
Bake for about 10 minutes but be careful not to overbake.
Cool on a rack before decorating with your favourite icing.

If you want to use these for decorating your tree, use a royal icing made with egg whites and flavoured with a bit of lemon juice.

Bigger cookies like gingerbread men will take longer to bake than small stars. For a pretty and crunchy cookie, sprinkle cookies with coarse sugar after icing.

BABY MOCHA CHEESECAKES

Chocolate and coffee is a flavour combination that almost always makes people swoon. These little babies are so nice to serve and just the right size for a small but irresistible indulgence.

- MAKES 12 -

CRUST

1/2 cup (125 ml) chocolate cookie crumbs
1/2 cup (125 ml) ground hazelnuts or almonds
2 tbsp (30 ml) sugar
3 tbsp (45 ml) butter, melted
1/2 tsp (2 ml) cinnamon

CHEESECAKE

1-8 oz (250 g) package cream cheese, room temperature
1/4 cup (60 ml) sugar
2 tbsp (30 ml) sour cream
1 egg
2 oz (60 g) good quality dark chocolate (callebaut), melted
1 tsp (5 ml) instant espresso powder*
2 tbsp (30 ml) coffee liqueur or 1 tbsp (15 ml) vanilla extract
1/4 tsp (1 ml) salt
12 chocolate covered espresso beans for garnish

METHOD

Preheat oven to 325°F (160°C).
Prepare a 12 cup mini cheesecake pan by greasing.
Mix cookie crumbs, nuts, sugar, melted butter and cinnamon together.
Divide mixture evenly among the 12 cups. Press the mixture firmly into the bottoms of the pans and about 1/3 of the way up the sides.
Place the room temperature cream cheese and sugar in a food processor or the bowl of your mixer and whip up until smooth and creamy.
Add the sour cream, egg, melted chocolate, espresso powder, coffee liqueur (or vanilla extract) and salt. Mix well to combine.
Put the mixture in a jug or measuring cup with a spout for pouring, or use a spring-loaded cookie scoop to get all the mixture into the 12 cups.
Place in the oven and bake for 15 minutes. The cheesecakes will puff up a little in the oven and fall when you cool them.
Remove from the oven and cool until set (about 30 minutes).
Remove from the pans by pushing up each cup from underneath then sliding a knife between the disc and the little cake.
Garnish with a chocolate covered espresso bean or a drizzle of dark chocolate.

A mini cheesecake pan is like a muffin tin but it has straight sides and removable bottoms. These pans make it so easy to remove the little cheesecakes and they look pretty and professional. The pans can be found at Cottonwood Kitchens.

*Instant espresso powder from Italy is a great addition to lots of good things in the baking world. It comes in little jars, lasts for a very long time and is available in Italian grocery or specialty stores.

STICKY TOFFEE DATE CAKE

Apparently the exact origins of this scrumptious English pudding are a culinary mystery. Our version is a cake brimming with dates, subtly spiced with cardamom and layered with gooey toffee sauce. It's a deeply delicious and comforting taste of days gone by.

- SERVES 10 TO 12 -

INGREDIENTS

12 oz (375 g) pitted dates, chopped
1 1/2 cups (375 ml) water
3 cups (750 ml) flour
2 tsp (10 ml) baking powder
2 tsp (10 ml) baking soda
2 tsp (10 ml) ground cardamom
1 tsp (5 ml) ground allspice
1/2 tsp (2 ml) salt
1/2 cup (125 ml) butter
1 2/3 cups (400 ml) dark brown sugar
4 eggs at room temperature and lightly beaten
2 tsp (10 ml) vanilla extract

TOFFEE SAUCE

2 cups (500 ml) whipping cream
1/2 cup (125 ml) butter
1 1/2 cups (375 ml) sugar
2 tbsp (30 ml) dark rum or brandy (or
1 tbsp (15 ml) vanilla)
1/4 cup (60 ml) pistachio nuts, shelled and coarsely chopped

You can make the toffee sauce well ahead of the cake, even a day or two. Just store it in a glass jar and reheat it a little in the microwave before using.

Serve with softly whipped cream or ice cream.

METHOD

Preheat oven to 350°F (180°C).
Prepare a 10 inch (25 cm) round cake pan by greasing and lining the bottom with parchment paper.
Combine dates and water and simmer over low heat for about 10 minutes until thick. Using a blender or a hand blender, process until smooth. Set aside.
Sift or whisk together the dry ingredients, flour, baking powder, baking soda, cardamom, allspice and salt. Set aside.
Cream the butter and brown sugar until light and fluffy. Add the eggs slowly with the mixer running. Add the vanilla.
Add the dry ingredients to the batter in three parts, alternating with the date mixture in two parts, mixing gently between each addition until batter is smooth.
Pour the batter into the prepared pan. Bake for about 40-50 minutes or until the cake is firm and a skewer comes out clean. Cool completely on a rack.

Pour 1 cup (250 ml) of the cream, all the butter and the sugar into a medium sized heavy bottomed pot and stir over medium heat until the butter is melted and the sugar is dissolved.
Turn the heat up and bring the mixture to a boil and let it simmer until it begins to turn brown and thicken up, stirring constantly with a wooden spoon for about 10 minutes.
When the sauce is golden brown and thick, remove it from the heat and carefully add the remaining 1 cup cream and the rum, brandy or vanilla.
Whisk it well until all the cream is incorporated. Simmer for a couple of minutes and remove from the heat.
When the cake is cool, slice it horizontally into three layers. Assemble the cake on a serving plate that will withstand a 200°F (100°C) oven.
Spread about 1/3 of the warm toffee sauce between each of the two layers. Finish the cake by pouring the remaining sauce over the top and letting it drizzle down. Sprinkle the chopped pistachio nuts over the top.
Warm the cake for about 15 minutes in a 200°F (100°C) oven just before serving.

TOAD MOUNTAIN GRANOLA

Yes, we do make our own granola here in the Kootenays and you will too once you try this.

- MAKES ABOUT 12 CUPS (3 KG) -

INGREDIENTS

5 cups (1.25 kg) large flake oats
1 cup (250 ml) raw sunflower seeds
1 cup (250 ml) white sesame seeds
1 cup (250 ml) whole almonds or hazelnuts, roughly chopped
1 tbsp (15 ml) cinnamon
1 tbsp (15 ml) ground ginger
1 cup (250 ml) applesauce
1/2 cup (125 ml) brown sugar
1/4 cup (60 ml) honey
1/4 cup (60 ml) maple syrup
1/4 cup (60 ml) vegetable oil
1 tsp (5 ml) salt
1 cup (250 ml) dried cranberries, blueberries or raisins

METHOD

Preheat the oven to 325°F (160°C).
Put everything except the dried fruit in a large mixing bowl and combine everything really well.
Spread the mixture out onto a large 12x18 inch (30x45 cm) baking pan. Do not line the pan with parchment paper.
Bake for about an hour turning the mixture over a few times during baking. You want everything to get evenly golden brown.
Cool completely before adding the dried cranberries.
Store in an airtight container.

You can substitute any kind of nuts or dried fruit that you like of course, and adjust the sweeteners to your taste, but don't leave out the applesauce. We think it's crucial for this granola's texture and taste.

LOG CABIN NUT BARS

Lakeside Physio owner Petra Lehmann shared these fabulous bars, loaded with a decadent combination of salty nuts and sweet caramel, they are full of crunch.

- MAKES ABOUT 24 -

FOR CRUST

2 1/3 cups (575 ml) all purpose flour
1/2 cup (125 ml) sugar
1/2 tsp (2 ml) baking powder
1/2 tsp (2 ml) salt
3/4 cup (175 ml) cold butter, cut into pieces
1 large egg, lightly beaten

FOR TOPPING

1/3 cup (75 ml) maple syrup
1/3 cup (75 ml) honey
1/2 cup (125 ml) packed light brown sugar
1/4 tsp (1 ml) salt
1/3 cup (75 ml) butter, cut into pieces
2 tbsp (30 ml) whipping cream
1 cup (250 ml) whole almonds, toasted
1 cup (250 ml) hazelnuts, toasted and skins removed
1 cup (250 ml) cashews, salted and roasted
1 cup (250 ml) pistachios, salted and roasted

These beautiful bars freeze well in an airtight container.

METHOD

Preheat oven to 375°F (190°C).
Prepare a 9x13 inch (23x28 cm) baking pan by rubbing with a little butter or spraying with cooking spray. Line the pan with parchment or foil to come up the sides of the pan. This will make it easier to remove the bars.

Whisk together flour, sugar, baking powder, and salt.
Blend in butter with your fingertips or a pastry blender (or pulse in a food processor) until mixture resembles coarse meal. Add egg and stir (or pulse) until a ball begins to form.
Turn out dough onto a work surface and knead once or twice.
Press dough evenly onto bottom of baking pan and bake until edges are golden and begin to pull away from sides of pan, about 15 to 20 minutes. Cool in the pan on a rack, about 20 minutes.
Bring maple syrup, honey, brown sugar and salt to a boil in a large heavy saucepan over moderate heat, stirring until sugar is dissolved. Boil without stirring for 2 minutes.
Add butter and cream and boil, stirring, for 1 minute.
Remove from heat and stir in all nuts until coated.
Spread mixture evenly over crust and bake until topping is caramelized and bubbling, about 15 to 20 minutes.
Cool completely in pan on a rack before cutting into small pieces.

INDEX

NOTES

also available, *Whitewater Cooks pure, simple and real creations from the Fresh Tracks Cafe.*
www.whitewatercooks.com, www.sandhillbooks.com